MW00677594

Book Five:

Maximum Saints
All Things Are Possible

Inspirational stories and drawings by incarcerated "Maximum Saints" and volunteers at Adams County Detention Facility, Brighton, Colorado.

Yong Hui V. McDonald

MAXIMUM SAINTS ALL THINGS ARE POSSIBLE

Copyright © Yong Hui V. McDonald also known as Vescinda
McDonald. All Rights Reserved.
Produced by Transformation Project Prison Ministry (TPPM)
All rights reserved. No part of this publication may be reproduced,
stored in a retrieval system, or transmitted in any form or by any
means – electronic, mechanical, photocopying, recording, or
otherwise – without the prior written permission from the copyright
owners.

All Scripture quotations are taken from The Holy Bible, New
International Version. Copyright © 1973, 1978, 1984
By International Bible Society. All Rights Reserved.

Printed in the United States of America
ISBN: 978-0982555170
Cover drawing: Rachel Marzullo, an inmate at ACDF
Cover Design: Lynette McClain
McClain Productions, www.mcclainproductions.com
First Printing: June 2012
TPPM is a 501(c)(3) nonprofit corporation.
Transformation Project Prison Ministry
5209 Montview Boulevard, Denver, CO 80207
Website: www.maximumsaints.org
Facebook: http://tinyurl.com/yhhcp5g

Adams County Detention Facility inmates have given their consent
to use their stories and illustrations in Maximum Saints books. Some
authors and artists names have been changed by their request.

All the proceeds from *Maximum Saints* books will go to TPPM to
distribute more free books and DVDs to prisons and homeless
shelters.

CONTENTS

DEDICATION

I dedicate this book to our Heavenly Father, our Lord Jesus, the Holy Spirit, and to all the incarcerated "Maximum Saints" all over the world whose hearts are serving Christ, saving souls and helping others.

Drawing "Dedication" by Burnie

Maximum saints are not necessarily classified as maximum inmates. I call them maximum saints because they use their gifts to the maximum to help others.

ACKNOWLEDGMENTS

My mother prays for me day and night. Because of her prayers, God granted me to see many miracles in my ministry. My gratitude to all the following generous people who donated their time and gifts to make this book possible:

(1) All the ACDF inmates who contributed their stories.

(2) Drawings: Rachel Marzullo, Burnie, Edger Perez and Letha Davis.

(3) ACDF editors: Don Burough, Cody Bushman, Francisca Cayon, Kathleen Cooper, Mary Diubaldo, Patricia Dowson, Danielle Engstrom, James Escalante, Brittany Espinosa, Rita Finney, Robert Garcia, Felonis Hernandez, Nadia Garcia, Amanda Gonzales, Bobbi Ignasiak, Joshua Langston, Irva Lenzini, Russett Loucks, Heather Lopez, Amy Low, Tiffany Lobato, Lisa Newberry, Arlene Pereda, Amanda Powers, Jennifer Richardson, Julia Roberts, Lupe Rubio, Eli Sandoval, Raelyn Santoya, Juanita Tamayo, Carmelita Taylor, Lakiesha Vigil, Mary Voogt, Christine Ward, Bernadette Warling, and Phyllis Wells.

(4) Volunteers who have helped with editing: Diedra Duncan, Tina Love, Janet Lysko, Amy Penn, and Bobbi Ignasiak.

(5) Art scans: Deputy Sheri Duran, Alvaro Duran and Jim Wickland.

(6) ACDF staff: Sheriff Douglas N. Darr, Captain Roger Engelsman, Melanie Gregory, Technical Services Manager, Mr. Sterritt Fuller, Program Coordinator and all of the Program Department staff.

(7) Donors: The following churches and individuals graciously supported the Transformation Project Prison Ministry through funding:

1) <u>Church sponsors</u>: Asbury Korean-American United Methodist Church (UMC); Brighton UMC; Broomfield UMC; Central UMC, Colorado Springs; Chapel Hill Church, Brighton; Columbine United Church; Cross Connection; Dover UMC; Faith UMC, Sterling; Frontier UMC of Cheyenne, Wyoming; First Love Healing Center; Fort Lupton UMC; First UMC, Fort Collins; Good Shepherd UMC, Thornton; Good Shepherd Community Church, Pueblo; Fort Morgan UMC; Grace UMC; House of Faith; Jefferson Avenue UMC; Korean-American Christ Central

UMC; Immanuel Mission Church, Denver; Community UMC, Keenesburg; New Gate Baptist Korean Church; Northglenn UMC; Love Outreach Pentecostal Church, Westminster; Paradise UMC, Paradise, Montana; Park Hill UMC; Peoples UMC, Colorado Springs; Resurrection Fellowship; Smoky Hill UMC; Stratmoor Hills UMC, Colorado Springs; Thornton UMC; Westminster UMC; West Lawn UMC, Pennsylvania.

2) Organizations and group sponsors: Church and Society for Peace With Justice from the Rocky Mountain Conference of the UMC; Duke Divinity School, Durham, North Carolina; Larimer County Detention Facility; Simpler Times; Metal Movers Towing.

3) Spanish book project sponsors: Marion and Lloyd Wake Human Rights Fund from National Federation of Asian American United Methodist Endowment; Rocky Mountain Conference of the United Methodist Church; United Methodist General Board of Higher Education and Ministry (BGHEM) Ethnic Concerns Committee; and Central UMC, Colorado Springs.

4) Individual sponsors: Jorge and Dan Adams; Pastor Richard Anderson; Edwyne Barney; Susan Bianco; Phyllis Blecha; Jack and Kathleen Bloom; Hyon and David Bohnenkamp; Tabitha Bonner; S.J. Bowman; Kenneth and Barbara Butcher; Jean Chase; Sara Choi; Martha Conant; Chaplain Sharon French from Larimer County Detention Facility; Franklin Feliciano; Pastor Yolanda Garcia; Carl and Linda Gardner; Kandis Glasgow; Kim Chun Il; Kim Woo Soo; Rev. Olga Jane Hard; Gerald & Marlene Hickman; Rev. Hugh Hazel Harris; Laura Nokes Lang; Dianne Lawson; Julie Lay; Alan & Marilyn Marquez; Rev. Donal Marxhausen; Flora Luz Movser; Sooja Oh; Pok Oke; Mark and Lori Osborn; Mary and Walter Oswalt; Nick Pacheco; Laura Padilla; Jon and Joey Prevo; Shari Quackenbush; Michael and Sue Rayphole; Delores Romero; Marcha Rotty; Joseph Saebi; Rosemary Samson; Theresa Sande; Phyllis Schultz; Joan Schwab; Rev. Rebekah Simon-Peter; Judy Smith; Dewayne and Robin Stephenson; Nieves Suarez; Debora Swan; Mary Trembly; Violet Winter and to all those who donated anonymously. Thank you and God bless you.

INTRODUCTION

Beauty Beyond Imagination

It's by God's grace that this book is available, so I thank Jesus for giving me the opportunity to be a part of this project. I have been so blessed with the *Maximum Saints* book project and prison ministry. I am in awe of what Jesus can do. Words are not enough to express my gratitude toward Jesus who helped me to be a part of the *Maximum Saints* book project. I praise God for all the dedicated God's people who are helping me with this book project!

Ministering to incarcerated saints has changed my life, especially the *Maximum Saints* book project. God has blessed me beyond my imagination. Among many blessings I have received, I will share one incident that I will never forget. I will say this is one of my mountain top experiences since I started working as a chaplain at ACDF since 2003. Also, this experience conformed to me why *Maximum Saints* stories are so powerful because their stories are stories of God's love and power.

In 2010, I went to ACDF on Thanksgiving Day to lead prayer in the women's module. As I was walking into the D Module, what I saw was not a beautiful sight. Some parts of the walls and floor needed painting; there was no way anyone could say that it was a pretty place. For the first time after I started working as a chaplain, I felt the beauty of that place so deep in my heart. I sensed it with my whole being. I knew it was a spiritual beauty that I was experiencing. This came from no one but the Lord.

Jail is a horrible, miserable and most sad place for many people. But that day what I was sensing was something I wasn't able to sense before. I understood that in God's view, it was a beautiful place. Jail is a place where God got many people's attention which was not possible when they were outside. Many broken people are seeking and trying to ask God for guidance and many are meeting Him and finding hope and healing. That's the reason I was feeling the beauty of the place. This is a spiritual hospital where the Holy Spirit brings healing in many people's hearts. I have seen many miracles on how God brought healing in people's hearts. Their stories are coming out and telling the world how God is helping them.

Who would have guessed that a revival is happening in the jails and prisons of America? I never guessed that I would see a revival in a jail. That's unthinkable but it is happening at ACDF. To be a part of this historic moment of revival in a jail is a privilege and honor. I am thankful that the Lord called me to be a witness of what He can do at ACDF.

One day I was leading prayer and meditation in Chaplain's Worship service. I had a spiritual vision that I was with Jesus. I was finding many precious beautiful stones all over the field like cactus growing in the desert. I knew what those beautiful stones represented. The beauty I saw in inmates who had experienced a transformation was like a precious treasure in God's kingdom. I am thankful that God was sharing His heart of how He saw treasured incarcerated saints—beautiful.

The Holy Spirit is blessing many people. Their testimonies are powerful. That's why *Maximum Saints* books are so powerful. With broken hearts, imperfect people, are talking about God's love, grace and power to transform. *Maximum Saints* stories have changed my life and many others in many different facilities.   One of the blessings I saw in 2011 is God opening the door for the *Maximum Saints* stories. Every week, transformation Project Prison Ministry (TPPM) received many letters from different prisoners from different States on how this *Maximum Saints* book changed their life and blessed them. But these books had been distributed only through chaplains, and were not available to the public. Every week, we receive letters with questions about how an individual can purchase the books or how outside families of the incarcerated can get a hold of a book. We have been receiving these inquiries for years.

In 2011, for the first time, God asked me to make *Maximum Saints* books available to the public so more people can be blessed by the stories. So, this book and other *Maximum Saints* books we published through TPPM will be available to the public. All the proceeds from *Maximum Saints* books will go to TPPM to distribute more books and DVDs to jails, prisons, and homeless shelters for free of charge. I praise God for His vision to reach out to more people through *Maximum Saints* books. God can do so much more than we can think or imagine with our testimonies, especially the stories of tears, pain and suffering. That's what the Bible is about: imperfect people's stories. However, God can bless them and use their testimonies to teach us. God uses our testimonies to bring healing in others as they read the stories and that's the work of the Holy Spirit. That's what's happening with the *Maximum Saints* books.

I am so blessed by the stories in this book and may God bless you as you read them as He has blessed me.

Chaplain Yong Hui V. McDonald

D

Drawing "Angels" by Letha Davis

Part One:
Testimonials

"They overcame him (the devil) by the blood of the lamb and by the word of their testimony." (Revelation 12:11a)

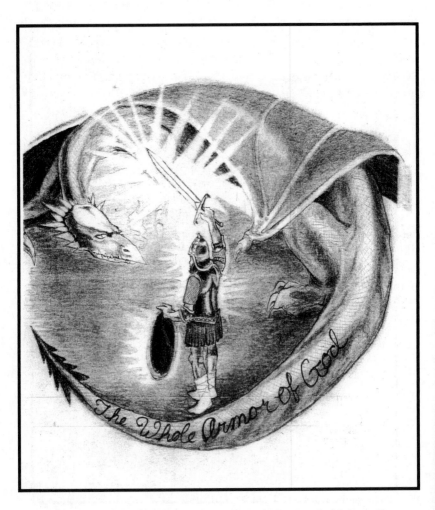

Drawing "The Whole Armor of God" by Rachel Marzullo

1. I FEEL LIGHTER — Peter Nguyen

I remember when I came to ACDF, I would see other inmates get called out to Chaplain's Worship each week. In my mind, I thought the guys were fakes because they're in here and wanted to be out of their cells. I remember calling some of the guys "Holy Men" because they would come back from church and read their Bible in front of me.

One day this inmate told me, "The more you make fun of them, the more the Lord Jesus will call on you." I would laugh at that, too. Then, a week went by, and I moved from F Pod to E Pod. I asked the deputy why I was being moved? They told me that I was going to be working with the Chaplain. At first I thought they were messing with me because of how I was messing with the other guys going to church. But it wasn't false; I was very angry because I didn't want to believe or be in E Pod; I didn't like being in the closed cell. Now, I had no choice, so the first week as a Chaplain's Trustee I was still in denial with God, because I was not into the religious stuff. So every day there I was still thinking about how to get myself back to F Pod; I liked to be outside.

As time went by, I started to read some of Chaplain McDonald's books and listen to what was said in church. I started to like what I was doing as a trustee. So, after 2 or 3 weeks of helping out as a Chaplain Trustee, a janitor named Ed stopped me in the hallway. He asked me to do something for a week. "Listen to the Holy Spirit each night for an hour, and you will hear the Holy Spirit."

Well, 8 or 9 days went by, and one night as I was doing that, listening to the Holy Spirit, I caught myself weeping a lot. So the next day I told Chaplain McDonald what happened. She told me it was the Holy Spirit. From that day on I started to feel lighter and happier, knowing that the Holy Spirit had spoken to me. I even stopped most of my cursing and all of my bad mouthing about the Lord to others.

What got me more motivated in believing is what's going on with Module A Pod 3 with the brothers. I feel that they are so powerful that each time I get to help in their group I become happy. Their testimonials were so powerful that they touched me. Now, each day and night I pray to the Lord about everything He has done for me. Especially now that I believe that He is our Savior. I thank

13

God for Chaplain McDonald, Chaplain Rick, Mr. Ed and all the A Pod brothers for helping me to believe in God. I can go home and feel lighter and more confident knowing that God has my back for the rest of my life. God is great and He is always welcome in my heart.

2. HE NEVER GIVES UP ON ME — Crystal Gillespie

I was in Pod 2 of D Module in ACDF. My cell mate left the facility and left a copy of the book, Purpose Driven Life by Rick Warren in the cell. I was a very devoted Wiccan at that time. I tried to avoid that book, but something kept telling me to pick up the book, so finally I did and read the first few pages. It caught my interest so I decided to read the book. It would only be 40 days and I surely had the days to waste. So, I read a chapter a day and at first it was just reading.

As the days and chapters passed, things in my life started to change, just little things, but very positive. Then God started to speak to me through the Scripture. And one day I felt the need to turn my life over to the Lord. Wow! The amazing things that happened! I was able to talk to my son on the phone when I hadn't heard his voice in five months. My court case started to come to a close, and I developed a very strong and positive support system.

I have never felt more positive about my life or more sure about the path my life was taking until the Lord forgave my sins. I started walking with Him.

Then on January, 15, 2009, I had the ultimate experience – I felt God put his hand on my shoulder! I was nervous, then I reached my hand up and placed it on top of His. Then I felt the Holy Spirit fill my body with such peace and love! God is great! He is so powerful and loving, so supportive, no matter what mistakes we make. My life is full now. I thank God for being there for me, for picking me up when I hit the ground, and for never giving up on me.

3. A WAKE UP CALL — Raelyissa Angelino Garnica

I am almost 30 years old. I'm not one of these kids who came from a bad or broken home. My childhood was very good, and both my parents spoiled me. In my early teen years I began running away and getting into trouble. When I was 16 years old, I got knocked up with my son Domenick. He was born at 26 weeks, weighing 2 pounds 11 ounces. He has had about nine surgeries. His dad went to prison for reckless manslaughter when I was 2 months along. Luckily I wasn't alone. I ended up with a good guy named Rick. He cut my son's umbilical cord and raised him like his own from birth. Eleven months later I had my second baby, Alexzandria, who was also a preemie with medical complications. So, here I am, seventeen years old with two kids.

I stayed with Rick for 12 years. Six years into our relationship we had our last baby, Adrian, who was born sick. I never was into drinking or drugs and neither was Rick. We bought our dream house, a 360k home in Reunion. I drove a Chrysler 300 and I owned my own business, "BubbleGum Blast Kids Center."

In 2006 we planned our dream wedding. To the outside world we looked envious, but behind closed doors we fought all the time. Six days before our wedding, let's just say it was cancelled. He went to jail. Yet I still stayed with him for two more years. In 2008, we split up. In a matter of months I lost it all! My business closed, my car was repossessed, my home foreclosed and Rick got custody and took my kids.

I was homeless with a bag of clothes and three boxes of pictures, memories, and my kids baby boxes. A so called friend let me stay with her and put my stuff in her storage. She stole about $2,000 from me and went to New Mexico; yes, I lost my stuff, my kids memories, and again I was homeless with nothing.

I thought I was so low it was impossible to get back up. I was shocked, thinking it could never happen to me. After that, I entered into severe depression. I didn't have my kids, they weren't coming back. So, to get my mind off of them and my problems, I turned to social drinking on the weekends with my friends. I found a new crowd and went from never doing drugs or drinking to drinking almost every weekend. It made me forget and helped pass the time. Drinking just clouded my thinking and made things so much worse. I was so overwhelmed with my life that I gave up and let it be controlled by the influences of other people and their opinions and drinking. I gave Satan control of my life without even knowing it. Look where that got me! In jail, and depressed, along with everything else.

Coming to jail was a God send. As miserable as it is, it's what I needed. I lost it all — cars, my home, my kids and now my freedom. One night in jail another inmate gave me the book, *Journey With Jesus*. I said, "I'm not gonna get into God just because I'm in jail." But I got bored with nothing else to do, so I read it.

Then, after I started reading a book, *Dancing in the Sky*, I was touched by an angel. Tears rolled down my face as I read about Chaplain McDonald's loss of her husband, Keith, to a car accident. Something inside felt different as the day went on. I noticed myself changing. I was literally reading two books a day and going to a lot of Bible studies.

The next morning, Halloween day, I was still sad. The Chaplain came in with a smile on her face that warmed my soul. We prayed in a group and she gave me some papers of her book to edit. I went back to my cell and thanked God for giving me something to do to pass the time.

As I began reading I realized God had sent this book to me. Not only to edit it, but to read it at this exact moment in my life when I was severely depressed and needed it the most. Everything I was going through was in this *Twisted Logic, The Window of Depression* book. I knew I was meant to read it.

Two days later the Chaplain came back, got the work, and gave me another book to edit. Again we prayed, but this time we talked and I told her my story. She invited me to write my story for her future books. I knew she was the sign I asked for.

Now I have a new perspective with God by my side. Here's what I have already gained and I know I have a lifetime more to come. God, Jesus, and faith to start. I gained knowledge that God took me from my materialist lifestyle and through all of that to free me from self glorification, all the no good, fake people who were in my life, all the negative. He saved me!

Being in jail isolated me from everyone and everything good and bad, even my kids. At first, and at times, I blamed God and was angry with Him, telling Him, "How could you do this to my kids? They suffered more than enough!" It was to show me how precious they are. I already knew, but He opened my eyes to it so much more.

Trusting in Jesus is all I need. He will provide for me all I need in this life. I know now it's not about what I have or do not have. I am still a work in progress and have so much to learn. But this I know; the things and life I used to want or have is over, and the new life I am starting is the total opposite. I just want to be humble and live a simple basic life with my kids. I am looking forward to a new life and journey with my kids and with the Lord. In just 45 days I can feel His power cleaning my soul, changing me every day a little bit more. It's like climbing a mountain: the more I get to know Him, the closer I get to the top and the farther Satan flees from me! I am no longer lost. Finding my relationship with the Lord has helped me find myself, my purpose and my future. The *Journey With Jesus* book and my own journey with Jesus not only changed my life, it saved my life.

4. CHRIST IN ME — Waymonn Boston

I was born in Denver, in 1956 and my childhood was pretty normal up until 1961. I grew up with a loving family and lived in a nice neighborhood, but everything changed when we moved to Westminster in 1961. Even though I was raised by spiritual principals and attended church regularly with my family, I had a hard time fitting in with other children at school and in my new neighborhood. It was difficult growing up as the only black family in a all white community.

Children can be very mean and I experienced a lot of prejudice at a young age. I covered my pain with anger, and became bitter and unforgiving. As I grew older, my parents told me that I had to be twice as good as the white kids, in order to be seen as their equal. So, I learned to work hard and I excelled in academics and in sports. I came to believe that I could achieve whatever I desired by "good works". This came to pass in all areas of my life except when it came to girls. Once I began dating, I was rejected by their parents and I experienced pain like I had never felt before. Along with the pain and bitterness, I felt ashamed of who I was and I felt unworthy of love. I didn't want to be different from everyone else, but I was and I developed a low self-esteem. Deep down I felt worthless and I desperately needed to fit in, so I began to drink alcohol and experiment with drugs.

My using began to change me. I hung out with a different crowd and acted out in order to be noticed. I found new courage and strength and I no longer took any crap from anyone, not even my parents. I became my own man. I stopped attending church and began to live my life. In high school, I was using pot and speed along with beer and wine, and I thought it made me better at everything I did. Soon I was off to college where I continued to use, but I couldn't see how it affected me until my grades slipped, and I lost my athletic scholarship. I should have seen the signs, but I was blind and could not see.

I came home and found a job and started hanging out in the clubs. I met the love of my life, so we moved in together and I set out to build us a rewarding life. Only the rewards I expected never came. Even though Debbie loved me with all her heart, the treasures of my heart were material things. After we were married, we bought a new car, a new truck, and a house, but I was never happy.

My using turned into addiction and my wandering eye turned into adultery. I hurt my wife in so many ways that all we did was argue and fight. Our marriage ended with the miscarriage of our twin boys, something I can never make amends for. Then I met a lady named Cocaine and for the next ten years, she took away all my pain. I loved her with all my heart until she turned her back on me. It was only after I received my third dope case that I tried to change my life.

I found myself at Peer-1, in an intensive treatment program. I completed the program and I worked very hard to stay clean and sober, but something was still missing. I continued to work at my trade but I was never satisfied. When I was an apprentice, all I wanted to be was a journeyman, and then life would be ok. But once I became a journey man, I envied the boss, and I wanted to become the foreman. So, I worked even harder and they made me a foreman, but my project manager made more money than I did and he drove a company truck. I knew if I could have his job, life would be good. A year later, I had his job, and a year after that I was field superintendent, but the happiness I was looking for was not in these jobs either.

All that was left was for me to run my own company, but not even that satisfied me. So, I went back to my old lover, that lady

Cocaine, but she did me dirty and broke my heart again. I woke up to find myself in the county jail again, facing my fourth dope case. I had nowhere else to turn so I thought I'd give God another try. I needed to find something that would keep me clean and sober and also fill the empty hole in the middle of my chest. So, I picked up a Bible and began to read and the Lord showed me what He wanted me to do. I was sent to prison in Walsenberg, Colorado, where they had a faith pod and I knew what I needed to do. I got into the program, and with the help of other inmates, I began to find God.

Then I met Charles Fredrick, who told his story in the first *Maximum Saints* book, *Maximum Saints Never Hide in the Dark*. With his love and guidance, I began to believe that there was still hope for me too. I got baptized and studied the Word day and night for almost a whole year. I obtained great Bible knowledge and I had faith the parole board would release me, and they did. I came back to Denver and was on fire for the Lord, or so I thought. But the world pulled me away.

All that Bible knowledge was useless in my head because it needed to make that 18" jump into my heart. Six months later I was back in prison and spent the next five years going in and out of jail and prison. Each time I was in, I studied the Word and vowed to stay clean and sober. But when I got out, I could only stay clean for a season. I tried with all that I had, but the power to do it, just wasn't in me.

After my fifth dope case, I was blessed with probation and I went to the recovery home at Victory Outreach Church. I began to realize that my recovery was about a relationship with my Creator and Redeemer. Looking back on my life, I never learned how to have a loving relationship with anyone. Needless to say, I didn't get along well with others and I became angry and frustrated and I ran away from the home. I stayed clean by working the 12 steps and I was so proud to pick up my one year chip, that I thought I deserved to reward myself. A week later I was using again. First I lost my job, then my apartment and it wasn't long before I was arrested for shoplifting.

God stepped in and rescued me, and brought me here to ACDF where I began to surrender. One day during the Chaplain's worship service, I received a revelation from the Lord. Pastor

Anderson was preaching from the book of Romans Chapter 7 and
the light came on. I began to see why I could not stay clean, no
matter how hard I tried. The things I want to do, I do not do and the
things I don't want to do, those things I do. He said, "It is not by
works, it's by faith. So stop trying harder and start trusting Jesus."
Then he took out a glove and laid it on his Bible and asked, "Can
this glove pick up this Bible?" "No," he said. "Not without a hand in
it." Neither can I do good works without "Christ in me."

At that moment my life changed. I understood why I was
baptized into Christ's death and resurrection. Jesus Christ died for
my sins, but he rose from the grave to live "in me," forever changing
me into the man God intended me to be from the creation of the
world. *Genesis 1:26* tells us that we are made in His image and
likeness.

Later that day as I sat in my cell meditating on His Word,
Jesus showed me how to yield to Him. He said, "Suppose your shirt
is your skin and your body is your will. Pull your arms in, from out
of your sleeves and step aside, turning 90 degrees without moving
your shirt. Now that I'm wearing your skin and you are out of the
way, we can do anything your heart desires. You just need to trust
me to lead you and promise me you will keep your eyes on me and
not on the world." Today I walk hand in hand with my Lord and my
God. He is the love of my life, the light unto my path and the wind
beneath my wings. He is Jesus, the risen "Christ-in me"!

For as long as I can remember, about once a month, I've had
a nightmare where the enemy is chasing me. I am running as fast as I
can, but my legs grow tired and weary. I have never seen the face of
the enemy but I can feel him gaining ground on me. Finally, I am
running in slow motion and right before he catches me, I wake up.
The last time I had this dream was two months ago, only this time I
saw his face, just before I got away. To my surprise, he was not that
scary.

I was then led to *Isaiah 40:28-31*. It says, *"Do you not
know? Have you not heard? The Lord is the everlasting God, the
Creator of the ends of the earth. He will not grow tired or weary,
and his understanding no one can fathom. He gives strength to the
weary and increases the power of the weak. Even youths grow tired
and weary, and young men stumble and fall; but those who hope in*

the Lord will renew their strength. They will soar on wings like eagles; they will run and not grow weary, they will walk and not be faint."

I felt like God had made a promise to me. He said in *Isaiah 40:29: "He gives strength to the weary and increases the power of the weak,"* and in *2 Corinthians 12:9,* God said, *"My grace is sufficient for you, for my power is made perfect in weakness."*

I give all praise to God, for He gave me victory over the enemy in my dream and I was able to escape. I woke up with such joy in my heart that I had to share my dream with my brothers in Christ. Because of the indwelling of Jesus Christ into my heart, I began to teach and preach the Word in our nightly Bible study. When I began to serve the Lord by working with others, the Lord gave me victory over the anger, hatred, bitterness, and an unforgiving spirit that once held me captive.

I received a great deal of help from the *Maximum Saints Dream* book. It helped me to recognize God's voice and that has deepened my relationship with Him. For years I have known I am in a spiritual battle and that Satan uses people to tempt me. I am either tempted into sin by anger and bitterness or I am tempted into sin by the lust in my heart. My Bible knowledge alone is not enough to fight the battle. I need the full armor of God!!

I put on His armor when I yield and surrender to Him in humble obedience. Each time I obey His voice, it becomes louder and I hear it more clearly. I want to be strong in the Lord and see His mighty power working in me and through me.

One day I had an altercation with another inmate. After walking away I felt embarrassed that I had been arguing and I felt grief in my heart. Instead of feeling anger and hatred towards him, I felt compassion and empathy for him. I was losing the spiritual battle and I could tell the enemy was gaining ground on me because I was having bad dreams again. I had to make amends to this man and forgive him in my heart.

The *Maximum Saints Dream* book helped me get my spiritual life back on track. Chaplain McDonald gave direction to putting on the full armor of God. She said, "The Lord is stronger than the devil so we need to be strong in the Lord." That's when I decided to memorize *Ephesians 6:10-18.* I believe having God's

Word in my memory is like never taking His armor off, so I can be ready for battle against the devil's evil schemes and his surprise attacks.

I learned to pay attention to my dreams because they show me my spiritual condition. When I am reading God's Word, attending fellowship and praying regularly, I have pleasant dreams. When I am being lazy and not reading the Word and not praying regularly, I have nightmares again. My life is so much better when I keep myself in fit spiritual condition. I give God all the praise and glory for the victory I have and for the man that I am today. May God the Father of Our Lord Jesus Christ give you His grace and peace!

5. IN HIS MAJESTIC SERVICE — Greg Lisco

Let me tell you about the wonderful things that God has done for me. I have been involved in going to church since I was very young. I was an altar boy most of my youth. We went to church (we kids that is) because Mom and Dad took us. It wasn't until I was 31 that I understood that God wants us to have a relationship with Him.

I was first introduced to Jesus in the Jefferson County jail. There I met a man who was there on a murder charge. He was a gang member and had been involved in the brutal murder of a young woman. What got my attention was his devotion and the persistence with which he was representing what he called the Gospel.

He told me that he was facing the death penalty for his involvement in this murder. He told me that he had made a deal with God. That if God would spare his life that he would commit to preach the gospel behind bars. He told me, "That we all have sinned and fall short of the Glory of God." He told me that the wages of sin is death but the gift of God is eternal life.

I would brush him off and argue with him. "How do you know God wrote that book?" I would say to him. You see, what I know now is that the appointed time had come, that all the prayers of my mom and her friends and all the prayers of my grandma and her church, were coming to fruition right there in that jail.

What I did not know is that the man of God was on his knees in his cell pleading with God on my behalf. He watered the seed of faith, praise God. He opened my eyes. My friends prayed with me and I accepted Jesus. Who knew that God would take that very thing that Satan sent to destroy you and turn it for your good. Isn't life awesome?

It was a day or two later that I was taken to Denver Reception Diagnostic Correction (DRDC). This was my first time through there. I must say that I was worried; I don't think scared is the right word. God had given me peace. I made it through the intake process. I was in the orientation room and found a Gideon Bible. I made my way to my cell and got situated. I sat there looking at my cell. I picked up the Gideon Bible and opened it. The first words I saw in God's words were *Hebrews 13:5b*. It says, *"God has said, 'Never will I leave you; never will I forsake you.'"* Praise God! Just what I needed and right when I needed it. *Ezekiel 34:26* says, *"I will bless them and the places surrounding my hill. I will send down showers in season; there will be showers of blessing."*

There I started the study courses which have given me the back bone of my faith. These courses will help you grow in your walk. They will teach you the truth as God wants you to know it. Of the 3 different facilities I was at, I couldn't help but notice that all were blessed by God and had wonderful bodies of believers.

The last facility I was in was Kit Carson Correctional Center known as Burlington. The church there was so alive and filled with the spirit that the guards would hear us praising God on the other side of the prison and come down to see what all the noise was about. Some would even fall to their knees with tears in their eyes, seeing the Glory of God and accepting Christ right there. The Bible says the Lord abides in the praises of His people. Just coming close to the presence of His glory will set a man free and heal a man's soul.

6. THE LESSONS — Donna Tabor

I was six months old when my mom was taken. I was there when it happened. My uncle killed my mother with a brick and there was blood everywhere. They tried to save her life but it was too late. My grandparents tried to raise us. Out of nine of us, I am the youngest. When I was one year old, I was sent to an orphanage called the Southern Christian Home. All of my siblings were there except my oldest brother. He stayed with my grandparents.

I was molested when I was seven years old, but no one believed me. I tried to tell, but no one would listen to me. When the people that raised me stopped working at the orphanage, I was devastated. I was 13 years old when that happened and I started to hate the world. I started getting high to kill the pain in my heart. I didn't want to think about what I had to do. I started abusing my body with drugs. I would sell my body for them; I went to jail when I was 15 years old. I thought that was love. I knew about Jesus and God but I really didn't know much about faith or having a relationship with God.

The lesson that I had to learn was that I had to let go and let God work in my life. Jesus started talking to me. But I was saying, "Who are you? How can I trust you? I have never trusted in you." He spoke to my heart. "I am not like any other man. I love you, Donna. I made you. I formed you in your mother's womb. I died for you." At that moment, I was filled with the Holy Spirit and fire. I was 22 years old and praying in tongues. Jesus touched my heart.

I do thank God for my life. I know He has a plan for me. The Scripture says, *"'For I know the plans I have for you,' declares the LORD, 'plans to prosper you and not to harm you, plans to give you hope and a future.'" (Jeremiah 29:11)*

How was I able to forgive my uncle that killed my mother? Again, the Holy Spirit started speaking to me, "How can I forgive you if you cannot forgive?" I had to let go and let God take control. My brother was in prison at the time. I went to see him and my uncle was at the same prison my brother was at. We sat at the table to see each other. My uncle was sitting at the table also and that's when the Lord spoke to me, "Now is the time." I started talking to him. He could not say anything. All he could do was look. It was time for the visiting to be over. We could take pictures before we left.

When it was time to say our good-byes, I walked over to my uncle and gave him a hug good-bye. At that moment in my heart I said to myself and God, "Jesus, I forgave him." I felt free in my heart. It has been very hard growing up knowing I would not see or talk to my mother. But the Holy Spirit, my comforter, started talking to my heart. I heard the Lord Jesus speak to me. He said, "You will see her." I was doing drugs to kill the pain. I do find peace with

Jesus. He is everything I need and more. Jesus is my Mother and my Father and my friend. Jesus, He is all and He is number one. He is that great. One of my favorite verses in the Bible is *Psalm 91:11:* *"For he will command his angels concerning you to guard you in all your ways." "A song of ascents. I lift up my eyes to the hills — where does my help come from?" (Psalm 121:1)*

My regret about being a parent was, here I am having children when I was 18 years old. I have three wonderful children. I put two of them up for adoption when they were four and five years old. I had to give them to Jesus. I could not do it any more. I got tired of dragging them here and there. They saw me being abused. It has been a long journey.

I know God can do anything. 14 years later I saw them for the first time, and oh what a joy. God can do miracles. He does miracles everyday if you only believe. I kept believing I would see them someday. I kept having faith. My 21 year old daughter has a son. I am a proud grandmother. My son is doing well. We still have to work on some things. In time Jesus will work it all out. I also have a nine year old and she does not know me. My relatives have raised her. I put my children in the Lord's hands and I know they are safe. *"I can do everything through him who gives me strength." (Philippians 4:13) "But seek first his kingdom and his righteousness, and all these things will be given to you as well." (Matthew 6:33)*

I believe in a God who has a great plan for me. It has been very hard to grow up without my mother. Jesus tells me she is my great angel watching over me. I want to tell my mother, "Thank you mom for having me." I know God doesn't make junk and I thank you Jesus for my life. I had a vision of Jesus and I do forgive my uncle. While I was writing this, I also had a vision of my mother flying like an angel in the heavens.

"Dear God, Jesus, I want to thank you so much for taking my mother into your arms. Thank you Jesus for loving me; holding me and taking care of me. Jesus, thank you for dying on the cross for my sins. Thank you for washing me clean in your blood. Jesus, I love you. My daddy, Jesus, you are everything to me.

7. HOW DID I FIND GOD — Adam Ramirez

It all started on February 15 when I finally got caught from being on the run from the halfway house. The Adams County police brought me here to this detention center. It all started when I went to Intake. The second day I was in there I saw a brother from the church where my grandpa preaches. He started talking to me about God. I've never been the type to talk about our Lord, but I didn't want to be rude, so I let him talk. Then I told him that I was going to call my mom – so please excuse me for a minute. And when I called, she told me that she'd been praying for God to send someone to bring me to Christ.

Every time my family tried, I would laugh about it, and make fun of them, and tell them that I didn't want to hear about that. So, I finally came to general population around 10:30 at night. The next day, after I got to my cell, I was looking around to see if I knew anybody, but there were no familiar faces. I was standing in front of my cell, and all of a sudden I saw this white guy standing there. I introduced myself and told him my name, and he said, "My name is Jon (Jonathan Willis)," and we started to talk. The first thing that came up was about our Lord Jesus Christ and in my head I said, "Wow, maybe there really is someone up there."

I had been here for three days, and everybody that I have talked to has been talking about God. I let Jon say what he had to say; then I walked away and went to my cell and thought about what my mom had told me. At that moment it clicked to me! So I dropped to my knees and asked God to forgive me and to come into my heart.

I started to talk to my brother Jon Willis every day. He was dedicated to the Lord, and I saw how peaceful he was – but it was Jesus I was seeing. I'm not saying that Jon is Jesus, but our Lord Jesus lives inside us, and I know God was using Brother Jon to get to me. I thank him for taking the time to fellowship with me and to show me what I've been missing out on!

I thank God for putting my brother Jon in my life because if I hadn't met him, I probably would never have found God. Now I really do know that God is up there, because He answers my mother's prayers, and the angel that God sent for me was Brother Jon Willis. There isn't a day that I don't pray for my brother, Jon Willis. He's family, because thanks to my brother, he saved my life from destruction and gave me the motivation to seek my Lord Jesus Christ.

8. HE ANSWERED ME — Mireya Vizcarra

Today, May 30, 2011, nearly 23 years have passed since my tragedy. At a very young age, I had the most terrible and painful experience of my life. I suffered both physical and mental abuse from the same man who would later get me pregnant. My pregnancy gave me the strength and courage to get away from him. I was in a place unknown to me and away from my family. I had been living in California for 23 years.

I gave birth to a baby girl. She made me feel proud about myself and was the reason why I wanted to keep moving forward in my life. My mother and sisters came from Mexico to welcome the new member of our family. Their hearts were full of love for my daughter. Two months after she was born, we were on our way to our first vacation in Mexico (my daughter, mother, sister and a cousin). We went on this trip and were very excited. I was driving.

My daughter was next to me and my mother was holding her. While I was passing through a little town between 5:00 a.m. and 6:00 a.m., I had an experience that I had never felt before. I felt like we were in a heavenly place, floating. Everybody was sleeping but my daughter and me. We were looking at each other, eye to eye. I never thought that would be my last time seeing her eyes open. She probably wanted to tell me that she would miss me and that she loved me, too.

Soon after I fell asleep, what felt like just a few seconds, all of a sudden I woke up, it was too late. Oh no! What happened next was horrible. I was trying to control my car which was already out of control. I have no idea how many times the car rolled over. When it stopped, the car was on top of me on the highway. People stopped to help us. I was fully conscious and concerned for my baby. I cried, "Please find my baby! Look for her! I am okay." They were digging a hole so my body would not suffer the pressure of the car. Why me? How? I couldn't believe all this was happening to me. I was in indescribable pain. Help arrived. My daughter and my mother were the first to be transported to a hospital by helicopter. My sister, cousin and I were transported to the hospital by ambulance.

My daughter was dead. My mother was in a coma, with only a 20 percent chance of survival. If she did survive she might be in a vegetative state or mentally ill. I was angry at God and asked, "If you really exist, why is this happening? Why am I alive? Why did I survive? Why am I not dead? That way I would not be feeling this horrible pain. Why? My daughter was the only reason for me to fight for life. She was taken from my arms." My suffering, grieving and pain wasn't enough. This was my fault. I am guilty. I was the driver. I killed my own daughter.

After three months, my mother responded. She was disabled, having suffered enough brain damage not to be normal ever again. Since then my anger was like a seed in my heart, growing. I didn't realize that the anger was covering my pain and tears. My personality and my character was changed overnight. I would not tolerate mistakes or wrong from anyone. I was hiding my grief, pain and anger. Focusing on succeeding in life, working many hours, and exhausting my mind and body.

My mother suffered for more than 18 years after the accident. When she passed away my anger grew. I didn't talk to any of my sisters anymore. Two and a half years passed by and I started reading a Catholic Bible; the Bible started to open my eyes and my heart. I asked God many questions. My understanding of Jesus' love, his life and his suffering was my breaking point.

Today He answered the questions that I had been asking Him 23 years ago. Why did I survive? Why was I alive? Why didn't I die in that accident? With a very loud, calm, kind and soft voice, He spoke to me. He had a purpose for me. His will for me in life wasn't done. He definitely wants me to tell others that He loves us, He forgives us and to forgive every single one that hurts us or has done something wrong to us. After understanding the real reason of Jesus Christ's crucifixion was to forgive all my sins, I was able to forgive myself and others as well. I started to change. That is when I learned to be humble and to have compassion for myself and others. Forgiving was my master key. Using it helped me to open a door that hindered me from walking to the other side and finding the real me: the person that God wants me to be, with a heart to use to love Him first and then others. I really love Him. I can't stop it. I am in love with God.

"My Daughter, my baby, I always wonder how you are looking at me. You and I had a very short time together and we know how deep those precious moments were. I still miss holding you in my arms. You know I told you to behave very good all the time no matter where we were. It was as if you always understood me. Well until today I miss having you next to me. One day we will be together for eternity. I love you very much and everybody in our family has a beautiful memory of you. They miss you too. We love you very much."

"To my beautiful Mother, You are in my heart and you will always be remembered. I have very beautiful memories of you. You taught me your ways very well. I see myself as a reflection of you. I love you very much. I am comforted to know how happy you are after suffering so much physical and emotional pain while you were on earth. I thank God for giving me understanding of your happiness when I see you in my dreams. Now you are healthy and are smiling and laughing in heaven. I just can't wait to be with you. I know we will have a great time singing and dancing for our King. I love you very much. I miss you even more. Just wait for me. See you soon, dear Mother." Your daughter.

9. ALL THINGS ARE POSSIBLE — Heather Waterhouse – Lopez

I am 30 years old. I was born in Denver, Colorado; my family then moved to Daytona Beach, Florida. I grew up in Florida until I was about ten years old. My parents did a lot of drugs, and my brother also did drugs with my parents. My dad was abusive with my brothers, and very emotionally abusive with my mother. He is the man, and the woman shuts up and does whatever the man says. When I was five years old, the neighbor would let me go play with his dogs. One day he molested me when I was six years old.

My dad and brother got raided when I was 12 years old. The F.B.I. and D.E.A. were on my roof and surrounding the house one night when I came home from roller skating. My dad and brother went to prison when I was 13 years old. My dad got a ten year Federal Prison sentence. My brother was 17 years old and he got a five year Federal Prison sentence for transporting Methamphetamines across state lines.

I was so lost after they took my dad. My mom lost everything and my other brother pawned all of my dad's expensive things. I ended up running away all the time and ended up in jail for three years at the age of 13. The judge and my mom said I was a threat to myself and society.

Here I am, 13 years old, with theft, joyriding, car theft, assault and battery, escape, drinking under age and lots more. Not good for a 13 year old. I was in and out of group homes. I made parole as a juvenile, just to be put in a home because my mom was strung out on meth, and using drugs with me.

My husband and I met when I was 11 years old. He was my best friend's brother. I was married to him from the time I was 15 years old and he was 29 years old. I have three beautiful kids by him, 4, 9 and 13 years old, two girls and a boy. They are my pride and joy. He gave me three angels out of the whole horrible relationship.

During 2005 he got out of prison. I was in a halfway house. We were together for the first time and I went to Denver Women's Correctional Facility (DWCF). I found out as soon as I got there that I was pregnant. While I was in prison, I was full term and slipped in the bathroom. I asked to go to medical but it took three days. I was bleeding and leaking fluid. By the time they saw me, my baby, Mikey, had died. I was in labor for 48 hours because he was dead. He wasn't moving down the birth canal right. The pain I was in, and the hate I had in my heart was so strong, it was indescribable—not to mention I was handcuffed and shackled the whole time. I got to hold him as blood was coming out of his nose and mouth. When they went to take him from me, I started screaming, "Wait, He is gonna wake up!" I cried, "Just wait!" They sedated me and sent me back to prison with a catheter. I couldn't urinate on my own. His little dead body had made me swollen.

When I got back to DWCF, all that people could do was tell me that they were sorry. A Chaplain came to me when I was in the hospital and asked if he could pray for me and the baby. I told him "Jesus isn't real. Why would God do this to me, why?" That's all I wanted to know—why? I lost all my belief then in the Lord. Even before that in 2002 my house was raided. My kids were taken right in front of me. They were screaming for me and I was screaming for them, it was the most painful thing I ever had to go through. I just didn't believe there was a God. Why would he allow such horrific pain and turmoil. I was molested when I was six, my father abandoned me, I had been locked up all of my teenage years, then the raid in 2002, and finally my Mikey dying. The psychiatrist diagnosed me with PTSD and manic depression.

I really would do well, but then when something bad would happen, I would resort back to using drugs and alcohol. I began using meth when I was 15 years old. I went from snorting, to smoking to I.V. using. I never thought it could happen to me. So, my kids (Thank Jesus) are with my family. This last time I did well. After I lost the baby in DWCF on October 6, 2005, they paroled me. I successfully completed parole and killed my number February 2008.

My husband and I bought a home, had three vehicles and everything was great. We also had our children back. My husband and I grew far apart because of his emotional and physical abuse. He has given me 36 stitches in my mouth. He held me and my son hostage in a basement with a Rambo knife to our throats. He said if I was going to leave him, all three of us were going to die. I hated him inside. I started using drugs again.

He went out one night and I found out that he cheated on me. So, I left him for three days. The next thing I knew I got a call that he had been arrested for assaulting a police officer. He had two and a half months left and he would have been off parole successfully. They gave him five years of DOC.

It's sad how you can be doing so well and you are happy one minute, then your whole world can change in a matter of seconds. There went everything we worked so hard for. He let the devil use him. The devil was already using me. He destroyed our lives again, in a blink of an eye.

So, I went back to using and stealing from the stores to pay bills, take care of the kids and feed my addiction. I started getting charge after charge. I was on a bunch of bonds, $150,000 altogether. I met my boyfriend in March and he brought me back to church and to the Lord. I felt the Holy Spirit in me that day. On January 5, 2010, we went to steal and everything went wrong. Now I am sitting here facing 16 to 32 years. I was bonded out for all these charges in

March. I got sick and had surgery, a stent was placed in my kidney and I missed court. Then I took off. My mother-in-law had my kids. I couldn't see them or have phone contact with them.

I hit rock bottom. I lost my kids, home, vehicles, husband and my life. So, we drove to Georgia first to see my mother who was sick. I wanted to see her before I went to prison, in case she passed. That was my fear. I blew all of the money on drugs and was so depressed. The devil was eating me up. Finally, I dropped to my knees and prayed. "Why me Lord? Help me. What do you want from me?" He wanted me to go back to Colorado. I was in Colorado's most wanted and there was a reward for my arrest. I was depressed, suicidal and a lost soul.

The FBI caught me on December 3, 2010. I was thankful for that, I was so tired of running. Now here I am and even though it sounds bad, I am okay because I have God and His son with me. They are carrying me right now. I have learned that without God, my world was out of control and unmanageable. I had to let go of my resentment, hurts, worries, angers, and twisted logic. I thank God for all the Christians He put in my life. God has given me the strength to go through my struggles and get through it with all the pain. I am smiling now. I still struggle with pain and nightmares. I rebuke Satan in the name of Jesus. My pain and tears will dry up. Nightmares are from my PTSD. My meds are helping, but what helps me more is prayer. God makes them go away.

Last week I was struggling. I was being ugly, hateful, hurtful and angry. I didn't feel worthy of going to the Lord in prayer. I felt like a fraud or a fake. So I went to my room and I cried so hard. I demanded God to answer me. I asked Him, "What do you want from me, Why? Why? Why? Are you there? Do you listen to me? I am a good person with a big heart. Why does my whole life have to be this way?" I never cried so many tears. Then I picked up the Bible and praise be to Him. He answered me and opened it up to this Scripture.

"You brought us into prison and laid burdens on our backs. You let men ride over our heads; we went through fire and water, but you brought us to a place of abundance. I will come to your temple with burnt offerings and fulfill my vows to you—vows my lips promised and my mouth spoke when I was in trouble. I will sacrifice

fat animals to you and an offering of rams; I will offer bulls and goats. Selah Come and listen, all you who fear God; let me tell you what he has done for me. I cried out to him with my mouth; his praise was on my tongue. If I had cherished sin in my heart, the Lord would not have listened; but God has surely listened and heard my voice in prayer. Praise be to God, who has not rejected my prayer or withheld his love from me!" (Psalm 66:11-20)

Each day is a struggle for me. Some days my faith is strong, and I believe everything is going to be ok in the end. The devil still gets a threshold on me. But I know the Lord's with me because in times of turmoil, He gives me answers. I feel the Holy Spirit when I pray. When I cry I can rebuke Satan in the name of Jesus and my tears dry up instantly. That's faith alone, just believing. *"I can do everything through him who gives me strength." (Philippians 4:13)* Today was a beautiful day. We were in the yard and this woman sang a gospel song so beautifully. I felt the Holy Spirit and I asked the whole group of women to gather in the yard, we prayed and we all cried. The Holy Spirit was with us all. We worshipped God together.

10. AMAZING DREAMS — Lakiesha Vigil

Have you ever had a dream that was so amazing you wish to have it every night? I've always had wild dreams…some funny, some that don't make any sense, and, of course, some bad. My roommate has told me she's heard me laughing, and even crying in my sleep. I actually love dreaming. It's different every night and I've got to tell you it is super interesting. Now before I share my amazing dream, let me tell you a little bit about myself.

I have been here at ACDF for a year waiting for trial. I am 21 years old and the oldest of three. My sister is 19 years old and my youngest sibling passed away in 1997. We were born and raised in Denver. My mom raised my sister and I alone. She did an awesome job taking care of us. My father has never been in my life. My sister and brother's dad was in and out of our lives.

I have been through a lot in my life — both good and bad. At seven years old, I was sexually abused by my sister's dad on a regular basis. Now I know you are wondering where my mother was while this was happening. Well, she worked two jobs to provide for us. The abuse lasted about two years. I never told my mom because he told me I would get in trouble. My mom found out when I was 14 years old. I haven't seen him in almost five years.

At 15 years old I became pregnant with my daughter. I left home to start my family with my baby's dad. I worked and went to school my whole pregnancy. I dropped out of school my senior year. At 17, I became pregnant with my son. Still I worked a lot. I had to provide not only for my daughter and myself, but also her dad; I took care of my sister and her daughter too. I did this by myself. I never had to ask for help and my girls never went without. I took on a huge responsibility for a 17-year-old, but I did it all with pride.

In July of 2007, I lost my baby boy. I was five months into the pregnancy. That's when I fell apart. I turned 18 and left everything I worked so hard for. I hardly saw my girls because I was always out partying. My little sister is the one who gave me a taste of reality. She cried and told me I was not her sister. That broke my heart into pieces. She said she didn't know or like the person I became. I was careless...irresponsible. I then realized I was not just hurting myself, I was hurting my family...my sister! So, I got my act right and found a job. I was back to being the girl I've always been known to be, the responsible, hard working girl.

In 2008, I got my first apartment for my girls. They had a home to call their own. All was well until August 25, 2009. My mom passed away leaving me and my sister alone. I completely lost my mind. I started drinking a lot, sometimes until I blacked out. I would run to my mom's empty house and pound on the door hoping she would answer and tell me it was all just a horrible nightmare. It was reality. She was gone and never coming back. I lost any kind of faith or love for God. He took both my son and my mom.

In February 2010, I was with the wrong people at the wrong time; I ended up here facing a lot of time in prison. This changed my life dramatically. I was housed in the medical unit for suicide observation. That is where I met Chaplain McDonald. I cried and cried to her and she listened without passing any judgment. She told me God had big plans for my life. She taught me to throw all of my fears, all of my worries, and all of my pain in a garbage can and leave it in the Lord's hands. Sounds easy right? There was one problem. I didn't know the Lord.

I got housed in D Module after I talked to the Chaplain. At this point I was in total shock. I was numb. I couldn't eat or sleep. I couldn't feel or think. I was just stuck. I read the book, *Maximum Saints Never Hide in the Dark*. As I read all the stories, I stopped and thought, " God really loves me!" I started attending Bible studies. I read my Bible every night and I prayed. I thought that was all I needed to feel peace. Boy, was I wrong!

Now let's get to the good part. January 25, 2011, I had the most beautiful, amazing dream ever. I was praising God, singing for Him in Spanish. Giving Him the glory He deserves. I was on a hill with green grass, big trees, beautiful flowers, and birds flying in the sky. It was an awesome view. I'd seen this incredibly handsome man dressed in a white robe. Remember I told you about losing my son? Okay, well, this man planted a seed in the ground. I watched it grow into a tall pretty flower. That seed was my son. As this flower grew I heard an angelic voice say to me, "Everything will be okay."

If you haven't guessed by now that man was none other than Jesus Christ. He let me see that my son is okay and grew up to be a handsome little angel. The Lord said Himself, "Everything will be okay." He gave me the honor to see Him face to face. He is real!

I believe He gave me this dream so I can put my trust in Him. This was His way of telling me not only is He real, He has the power to heal a broken heart. Like a real father, He was there to pick up His daughter when she fell and healed her scrapes.

As I sit here sharing my story with you I am still learning to trust God. I am far from perfect. I still have a lot of growing up to do, but I have faith that can make mountains dance. I know my Father will help me get on the right path. Only He knows what's best for me. I am only a mere human, who am I to question my Creator? The Scriptures confirm that He only wants what's best for His children.

"'For I know the plans I have for you,' declares the LORD, 'plans to prosper you and not to harm you, plans to give you hope and a future.'" (Jeremiah 29:11) "Trust in the LORD with all your heart and lean not on your own understanding; in all your ways acknowledge him, and he will make your paths straight." (Proverbs 3:5-6) All He asks is for us to confide in Him. Now, I don't know about you, but these Scriptures speak loud and clear to me. God is

great! He loves us no matter what we have done. Seek the Lord with all your heart. He will never give more than we can bear. Have faith the size of a mustard seed and watch what our Heavenly Father can do. May his will be done. God bless you.

11. JESUS IS COMING — Bryan Sandoval

In my life I have had a lot of dreams as well as a lot of nightmares. Sometimes I believe dreams are instant messages of the future or messages you need to change the will of. I believe the Lord gives us the choice to do what's right or wrong. I know He designs paths for us to walk, but we choose to walk with God or walk with the enemy.

I have been at ACDF for three months now. I've had a lot of strange dreams, but I've had the most religious dream of my life just recently on February 20, 2011. I prayed really hard as I do every night. On this night I asked God, "Give me a sign to show me what I need to do to make it to the kingdom of heaven." So, I had this dream where my brother and I were at this house, a very nice house, with these people that I didn't know.

My brother and I went outside and I looked up in the sky and all I saw was a red horse with a saddle running through the sky as if it were on the ground. I immediately starting saying, "Jesus is here. Jesus is here." Behind the horse were three horses, another red horse, a black horse and a white horse and five birds that looked to be pigeons, though I am not sure. From a distance I could see all the people of the town in the streets on their knees with their hands in the air to the horse. Then, the black horse was in front of me. It kept trying to fly, but it could not. Then it stood staring at me with anger. I was very scared, so I just stood there and then it left me alone.

I woke up in amazement; shocked that I just had that dream. I believe the Lord Jesus is telling me that, "We need to repent and surrender to the Lord because He is coming!" I think the black horse represents Satan being jealous because I knew Jesus was here and he didn't want me to feel the love of God that I felt as the red horse ran above me. The devil wants to bring us down any way he can get us down. We have to put the full armor of God on and be ready to battle with the enemy. *"He who testifies to these things says, 'Yes, I am coming soon.' Amen.*

Come, Lord Jesus. The grace of the Lord Jesus be with God's people. Amen." (Revelation 22:20-21)

12. A GUARDIAN ANGEL — Mary Voogt

I am a mother of three wonderful boys. However, that all changed when I lost my youngest son Issac. December 21, 2009, he was 12 years old and in his first year of Jr. High. As we all know, this part of growing up brings new friends, new experiences and new peer pressure. Issac, like any other 12 year old boy, just wanted to fit in.

Issac was the class clown. He enjoyed making people laugh, but it got him suspended. On December 14, at the time he lived with his father Greg, his consequence for this was getting his new bike taken away for one month. He stayed home alone and had his own set of keys and a cell phone. He always answered his phone, if he missed a call, he was sure to return the call immediately. The first time he didn't answer or return his father's call, that quickly brought an alert to Greg. He headed home, continually calling Issac, but getting no answer.

When he arrived home, he couldn't find Issac. As Greg headed for the door to go out and look for Issac, something kept telling him to push the closet door open. He found Issac, he had hung himself. In a panic, Greg tried CPR to revive him but he was completely unconscious. Greg cried out for help. A neighbor called 911. The ambulance arrived to take Issac to Denver Health. Upon Greg's arrival to the hospital, the chaplain called and told me I had to get to the hospital.

As I rushed to the hospital my initial thought was that Greg had attempted suicide. I never imagined my son, Issac, would try to take his own life. When I arrived at the hospital, I went to the front desk and requested to see my son's father. I thought he had attempted suicide. The receptionist looked a little confused and told me my son's father was coming from the elevator with the chaplain. Greg was hysterical. His only words to me were, "I don't think he's going to make it, Mary." I fell to the floor in total shock.

As I walked into the hospital room, I saw my son lying in the bed. Not knowing whether he would live or not had me dumbfounded. The doctor then explained Issac's condition to his father and I. His brain cells were slowly dying which may result in Issac being brain dead. He fought for his life for a week or so. In that week he opened his eyes when he saw his older brothers, and he reached for their hands. That was the only reaction we had gotten from Issac. The hours of each day slowly went by. We had a lot of family support and many prayers.

December 16, a couple, Jenny and Mark, arrived claiming they had been sent by God for Isaac to speak to his mother. I prayed with my two sons and Jenny and Mark. As Jenny began the prayer we held our hands over Isaac. Suddenly the entire room grew so bright that I couldn't open my eyes. The Holy Spirit then began to move through my body. I could feel my breath almost being taken. I had a vision of large hands holding my son in the clouds. Jenny then said to me, "Mary, Isaac has already gotten a touch of heaven. God has opened the gates to His kingdom."

My two older sons and I then felt at complete peace. A huge weight was lifted from our chests. The Lord took away all of our pains and worries. I worried about where my son would spend eternity, silly me. I knew he was now in the kingdom of heaven where he was given the unconditional love that only our Father can give and the eternal life He promised to us. Knowing that was the best feeling for my boys and I.

We were covered with the blood of Christ. The enemy can no longer take anything from me or my boys. That alone was a blessing. My little boy is now our guardian angel. If you have ever experienced what the Holy Spirit can do then you know there is no greater power. The Lord works in mysterious ways. I truly believe having the vision of my son was a gift from God. He showed me Isaac was in paradise as happy as can be. I'm sure he is making God's angels laugh, non-stop. "Thank you, Father God, for giving me the privilege of loving one of your precious angels. Thank you for your endless love Father." We love and miss you, Isaac.

13. FORGIVENESS — Sabrina Mitelea

I truly had no clue what a toll not having a father really had on my life until I was 18 years old. I was living a life of pure hell inside myself. When I was 12 years old my life was shattered by a single drunken night my father engaged in. He drank himself into oblivion and proceeded to tear my shirt off of me trying to get me to have sex with him. I cannot begin to tell you how this affected me as I was a daddy's girl like no other, my world was woven around him. We were inseparable.

Out of desperation and fear of dreaming about these events, I tried any and everything to stay awake. I experimented with any drug I could get my hands on, and finally I found the one, my cure, crystal meth. I was finally able to cope with my life. Because of my lack of sleep and my self-esteem I had quit school. I was in 8th grade.

I started running away, partying and having sex with several boys. I'd even taken my big brother with me when I ran away. He started doing drugs with me and drinking very heavily as well. He was so innocent and so good, but I was selfish and didn't care. I wanted the world to feel my pain. I'd turned on my poor mom and my whole family. When I was 13 I ran away and to this day have not returned home.

I actually enjoyed seeing other people's pain and suffering. It made me happy for people to know I was the one who had hurt them. I had nowhere to turn for help. God didn't even exist at that point of my life. I was alone and pure evil.

This went on until Feb 21, 1991, the day I had my little boy, the day I got my heart back, somewhat anyway. I remembered how to love someone again. This was huge for me, although I was very hard and frigid still. With as much joy my son brought to my life, there was something missing. I kept trying to fix myself with drugs, sex, and alcohol but to no avail.

When I was 18, I had my oldest daughter. For three years as I watched my two precious babies grow, my resentment for my dad just grew. Not so much resentment but hatred. I truly wanted him dead. I had even inquired about poisoning him several times in the prison years.

I resented him for missing out on watching my kids grow and them missing out on him teaching them how to ride a horse or listening to him sing or his stupid stories about how he saved them from the Milky Way in the sky. All the things he did with me they were missing and it wasn't fair.

I felt like he had robbed me of any chance I had of a normal life. I was pregnant with my second daughter when I got a knock on my door at 5:49am one day. It startled me as I was not expecting anyone. I opened the curtain and was stunned to see my dad and uncle standing on my porch. I have no clue still how he found me as I had not spoke to his side of my family for six years for fear of this very thing happening.

My son ran up to the door as I stood there in shock and looked at my dad and said, "Papa." That was an act of God as I certainly never mentioned him to my kids. I felt a jolt that kind of made me just reach out and open the door for them. Believe me, that was not my initial intention.

Something inside of me knew instantly what I needed to do, what was missing was forgiveness. I needed to forgive my dad for what he had done so many years earlier. It was God that made me forgive him because that idea never even crossed my mind. The Lord touched my heart that morning and made forgiving my dad possible, and because of Jesus, my dad and I have a good relationship today. He was around to watch me raise five children, and I thank God for that daily. I love my dad. Thank you Jesus. I love you for teaching me how to forgive.

14. FROM VICTIM TO VICTOR — Georgette Wires

When I was a little girl, I was abused in every way possible. Being physically abused hurt me more on the inside than it ever could on the outside. It seemed the only "attention" I got was when I was being sexually abused. After a while that all became normal. So normal, that by the age of ten I was being pimped out by my aunt. I remember being so scared the very first time, but I had already developed the "people pleaser" mentality so I didn't want to make her mad. My mother was a disciplinarian and a workaholic so all the things that went on with me she never knew until 2007.

Debbie was supposed to be babysitting me not pimping me. After two years of this she introduced me to cocaine at the age of 12, which I would end up battling for the next 26 years. I was hitting the pipe with grown men who, in turn, began to use my body as their playground. Somewhere deep inside of me I knew all these things were wrong, but after awhile it all became twisted and I thought it was normal. Growing up around pimps, hustlers, and drug dealers, it seemed my destiny to become a part of the streets. I didn't get tossed into them, they were embedded in me. All the while living a double life, because at home I was a daughter with no affectionate connection to my mother. I was teased at school in the projects because I was a half breed so, therefore, I was born a misfit. Not ever being able to fit in anywhere, only with my aunt and her "friends."

I was given up for adoption at birth because my biological mother got pregnant when she was underage. I battled the issue of abandonment for a long time. Somewhere throughout all this, my mom, my Grandma, and I went to church every Sunday. Once I began to get older, I began to hear "God is love," "God loves you," "Jesus loves you." I remember questioning it because if He was near, why was my life so full of pain and hurt? Did He not like me either?

At 15, my dad passed, which didn't mean too much to me because he had done his damage too. When I was seven my dad moved his mistress into our home destroying everything my brothers and I knew to be normal. To this day I don't know how my mother came through and still remained sane. She took me and my brother, Sam, and moved out, which opened the door for more abusers. Babysitters who would beat me crazy, one even burned my arm with scalding water. For whatever reason, I was always taught to believe that I was bad and unwanted. There were wounds that would scar me and become oppressive holds on me throughout life.

My mother and I moved to Colorado. Her cousin lived out here and they were "super sanctified." Something I didn't know about. They were strict, mean, and abusive, but "churchy." So, I went from playing the role of an adult from 10-15 and doing adult things, to no freedom, wearing dresses, being in church, and missing my home in Illinois. I was a sad fish out of water. I wasn't getting with the program due to "street mentality."

I once again got the hell beat out of me! It was so severe the neighbors called the police and when they came I told them I was alright because I didn't want to leave my mom. Well, instead a short time later I met a pimp (how ironic) and ran away with him. Nobody ever came looking for me. I was with him three long months. Everything my aunt had taught me, the ante, just went up, because it went from bedrooms to street corners all across America. Then the beatings began and I didn't understand. So I ran away from him and made my way back to Colorado. My mama let me in, but to my surprise she never asked one question. I began to believe she didn't care. Years later I figured out that she just simply didn't know how to care. After getting back here, I met a high-profile hustler and he became my entire world until I got pregnant at 17. He got me on cocaine and everything began to change. He began beating on me, leaving, and staying gone, all the while making me believe it was because of me. After two babies, I entered prison at 20, took a 3 year sentence and turned it into 20 years. Through the next 20 years, I would enter prison, get out, after two weeks free I would relapse and be on the run, only to return back to prison. During my relapse, I would get involved with men who took abuse to a whole other level. I have been beat, burned, stabbed, and left for dead by men I thought loved me.

The abuse was normal to me because I didn't know anything else. To me it was love. All they had to do was say, "I love you" and they had me. My last relapse ended up being my worst (2007). I hated myself. I hated who and what I had become. I didn't want to go any farther. So I figured if I kill myself, I would be easing everybody's pain. Well, I didn't succeed, and in my frustration of not being able to even do that right, I began to cry out to God like I had never did before.

I knew about Jesus, I even had a relationship with Him. He had a special kind of way of dealing with me. Only in jail would I seek him. He always made himself known to me, but when I got out of jail, I would leave him at the door. Never intentionally, of course. I wanted to know what was so wrong with me, why couldn't I ever get anything right? My life had become a series of failures. I couldn't begin to understand the way of it all.

If you don't know you are broken, how do you know you need to be fixed? Because of all that happened, I had developed deep wounds that over time had become buried. It seemed with each incident the scab would be pulled off and more salts would be poured into me. Pain that sometimes felt as if someone took my heart and decided to scrape it raw. How could I even begin to tell anyone what I was feeling when I couldn't describe it to myself?

A feeling of loss, hoping to be found but not knowing how to say help me. When it hurt, I would get high. When I got high, I would run, and I ran right back to the arms of the streets, where for some reason I felt accepted and wanted, only to quickly become a victim of more abuse. How does one become a mother of eight beautiful children and not even know how to mother them?

Here's a better question. How does one become an adult and not know how to function as an adult? Well, that was me and that was my story. All I felt was the hurt, pain, and heartaches of the people that said they loved me. All I wanted to do was be that little girl again and run and hide somewhere I couldn't be found. But really, I wish somebody would have found me. I wish someone would even come looking for me. But for years and years no one ever came. As time went on either I found myself on the streets or in a jail cell.

All I wanted was someone's arms around me, someone to sit with me, and talk to me, letting me know they understood. For some reason everybody always thought I needed tough love. Today I disagree. Tough love, unfortunately was something I already knew. To me it says: lonely, outcast, you don't belong here, you are not good enough, you disgust me, beat me, hurt me, you don't deserve good things, you will never amount to anything! When people are in pain, you don't beat and badger them down more. I was so out of touch, when my mother did try to reach me, I was too far gone. I had built a thick wall around my heart, not even realizing it or knowing the how and why of it. I didn't even believe my own mother loved me.

Years later I came to realize that even if she never said it, her actions always spoke way louder. She always had my children and she never turned her back on me. I just didn't know how to say, "I'm so heart sick, and full of bullet holes."

Who can help me? Through the years, I learned that there is only one who could help me. His name is Jesus! And I only became acquainted with him in jail. One thing about him, he has never abandoned me. No matter what I've done or where I've been. Even when I left him behind, he is somebody that never gave up on me. At 15, I didn't understand who Jesus was and how he could be so gentle and kind. When I first began my walk with him, it was so lovely and nice I never wanted him to leave me. I didn't understand that in order for him to stay with me I had to stay with him.

I left him many times and each time my pains got worse and worse because now I had been introduced to guilt and shame. It made me sad even more so because I knew I had let him down. I had to learn that once you repent and ask for forgiveness, he is not like man, he really forgives you. He began to take each heartache, and the pain that was connected to it, and started the healing process. With each hurtful memory he took away the sting that was connected to it, all the while showing me the deeper meaning of forgiveness. Forgiving my abusers then forgiving myself. In that, freedom has come.

Sometimes the enemy will tap at me and begin to accuse me all over again. He will try and tell me how unworthy I am and all that comes with it. In my mind I have learned that is where the battle begins. The more I study God's Word, the more I have to fight with. Through all of my failures and all my falls, Jesus has been right there, without stretched arms waving me back to him! With Him, I don't have to explain because he already knows about it. It is so much relief—just giving it all to him. After 17 years I finally understand that he wanted a surrendered heart—my heart where my free will lies. All these years I had been saying, Lord I give you my life. Well I get it now, my life is something he already has.

Folks say walking with Jesus is a journey. It really is! I used to want everything right now. With Him, change doesn't happen in a right now way. With every fall, in my getting back up, I have learned something different every time. Most importantly, he will never leave me nor forsake me. He will come to me and not leave me an orphan. He is a true living God and his Word is living and powerful. Life with him just gets better and better, no matter how alone I may feel, no matter how dark it may get, and no matter how strong the storm, I know he is there. His love holds me, surrounds me, and encourages me and all that I've gone through is just the preparation for His purpose in my life. *Romans 8:28* says, *"And we know that in all things God works for the good of those who love him, who have been called according to his purpose."*

And yes, we are all called no matter where you have been, who you are, or even where you come from. Our lives have purpose and meaning all with God getting the glory. Please don't give up and definitely don't quit. The greater the struggle, the greater the triumph. The power of Jesus Christ knows no limitations. My sins, my failures, and my mistakes are somehow weaved into the tapestry of my life and God makes no mistakes. He loves us all, one and the same. His mercy and compassion are truly real and he never changes. He really is the same today, tomorrow and forever. Please open your hearts and call on him. He will answer, and he is already waiting. Jesus loves you.

15. WALKING WITH GOD — Edger Perez

Praise the Lord Jesus Christ for allowing me to share my testimony. I am 31 years old with three children, one daughter and two boys. I am a permanent resident originally born in Zacatecas Mexico in a little Rancho called La Noria De Molinos. My parents first brought me here to the United States when I was just a two month old baby, along with my older brother and two older sisters through the border illegally. It was hard for me to believe it but it was true I was that young.

I grew up in North Denver in my younger years in poverty and had a rough outlook growing up because of it. The Lord blessed me with the skill of being an artist and my skill evolved as the years passed. I tried to find myself in spiritual philosophy called the Bhagavad Grita which I had to let go of in due time because I still felt a void and sensed it was meaningless. I found myself then getting into alcohol and drugs coming in and out of jail, having problems with my relationships, getting good jobs and losing them because of Mr. Vicious Cocaine.

The first encounter with the Holy Spirit I had was when I was in Denver County jail. All year it was fresh. All of our morning Bible studies we had were powerful. We had an evangelist and a disciple in our Bible studies. Then one night the Lord blessed me in a dream with the Holy Spirit.

In the dream a brother that was in our group and I were sitting at a table in the facility, conversing, then suddenly he told me, "Let me pray for you brother." Putting his hands over mine and placing his right palm on my forehead, he commenced to pray, then boom, a sensation of light and a warm feeling tingle struck my

whole body from my head down to my feet. I felt something
tremendous, something I never felt before. Amazing for real!

16. THANK GOD FOR USING ME — Justine Lenzini
    In January, 1998, I was sentenced to DOC—prison—for 20
years; but that is another story. What happened afterwards is the
testimony I wish to share. See, all of the others who were sentenced
around the time I was, had been taken from ACDF to another DOC
holding facility within two weeks of their sentencing. It had been
almost two months and I was still here. Why? I was a newly born
again Christian, hungry to read the Bible and eager to obey God's
word. So, I figured there must be a reason for the delay in my move.
Still, I was questioning it. Then in early March, as a few of us, who
read Scriptures early in the morning were talking about what we
read, a woman came in with her box and went into the cell next to
mine. No one really paid any attention because this was jail, new
people come and go all the time.
    Today proved to be different. Within less than half a minute,
the woman came back out. She was upset and very pale. She cried
out, "Someone has hung themself in my cell!" I don't recall exactly
what my thinking was, but as everyone else ran around yelling for
deputies, screaming for help, or running to their own cells to hide;
my feet took me straight to the cell with the would-be suicide
attempt. I had taken CPR and first-aid and was certified at one time,
it was expired though. Still, I remembered clearly how to deal with
this situation: support the neck and head, remove the "rope" (a sheet
in this case), gently lower the victim, check for breathing and
perform CPR if necessary. It had been over two years since I'd taken
that class, why was it so crystal clear this day? And why hadn't I
panicked? I knew I was scared. I can only attest that God had used
me to help this woman. I did as I remember, step by step; and as I
was about to perform CPR a deputy came in. He said, "I'll take it
from here, Ms. Lenzini. You just go lock down." I did as he had told
me. Then I did as God told me—I prayed for the young woman who
had tried to take her own life. I prayed and I cried for her life as if
she were family, when I didn't even know who she was.
    About 45 minutes to an hour later, the deputy came to my
cell door. He said he wanted to thank me for what I had done,

because if the girl had to wait for him, probably her brain would have been damaged, due to the lack of oxygen. Whereas, my already having let her down from the tether, she was going to be just fine. I broke down and cried, thanking God for the woman's life. I later found out she was a young mother whose children had been picked up by social services. She thought it was the end of the world. I was told she got counseling and was now happy to be alive.

Now I know that was God's purpose in my delay from leaving ACDF. I say this because I left two days later! Even to this day, I am not certain why I did what I did. I'm not what I would call a brave or even assertive person. And what I recall, to me, seems more like remembering a movie I had watched—like it wasn't me that had done that. I truly believe that the Holy Spirit took over, so I give all glory and praise to God for saving that young woman's life. I thank God for using me, and giving her and her family a second chance at life. I still pray for her and hope she has turned things around.

This experience helped me about a year and a half later, as I felt like my world had come to an end. I was depressed by a letter from my child that hurt me severely. I had wanted to end it all, too. Instead, I cried out to God and He reminded me of the relief everyone in our pod had knowing the woman had survived. They cared. Someone always cares. You may not know who, but there is someone out there who is praying for you. God kept me from attempting suicide that day because I didn't want anyone to find me—like we had found that young girl. I realized then that suicide hurts everyone who comes in contact with it. No one wins, except Satan—who comes to kill, steal and destroy: he kills through suicide; he steals joy and the life that was possible; he destroys all the good that the victims of suicide may have done with their lives.

I have totally turned my life over to God. My 20 year sentence now has less than nine months left to it and I have done that time in service to God. I hope to share more of the testimonies of how He has changed my life for the best and of all He has done for me.

For those who have thoughts of suicide–please, seek out help, even if it's someone who will pray with and for you. Pencils have erasers and nothing is worth letting Satan win even one day of

God's precious gift of life. I've heard that many suicide survivors have said they changed their minds after it was too late. They lived to remember that. So, take time to seek help, and you won't go through that. I've also heard that threats of suicide are a cry for help. Take all threats seriously and be part of the solution—even if all you can do is pray, it's what you should be doing! Trust me—I know.

17. MOMMY LOVES YOU — Amy Low

I am writing this in hope to help someone who is going through the same thing that I am. I am 21 years old and have two sons. Tanner is three years old and Michael is three months. I *came to* jail July 2, 2010. I was three months pregnant when I was arrested. This was the first time I had ever been to jail. You can imagine how scared I was. I didn't know where else to turn so I crawled my way back to Christ.

I prayed everyday that God would give me a miracle and give me another chance to do right so I would not have to have my baby in jail. It was because of my own stupidity, selfishness, and my addiction to drugs that Tanner was taken away from me.

I spent day and night hating myself for letting my son, my own flesh and blood, go through the things he went through. When I was three years old, I was taken away from my mom and put in foster care because she was addicted to heroin. I was adopted when I was five years old with my sister who was three years old at the time. I was very close to my adopted father but not so close with my adopted mother. My father died of cancer when I was 11 years old. My mother and I just could not get along. I ended up moving out when I was 16 years old and have been on my own ever since. The last thing I ever wanted to do was put my son through the things I went through when I was young.

I thank God everyday that my aunt and uncle adopted Tanner when my rights were terminated. I still don't get to see him, which kills me more than anyone can comprehend, but I know that he is safe and loved.

Anyway, court date after court date went by and each time they gave me a new court date. As it got closer and closer to my due date, I started to lose hope, and even started to get angry at God for making me go through this. I had already lost one son, how could He let me go through this pain and heartbreak again? I spent the last three months of my pregnancy running from anything spiritual. I felt so alone and abandoned. I did not know how I was going to get through this. I hated spending my whole pregnancy, which is supposed to be a happy time, being scared and not knowing what was going to happen.

I didn't want to get attached and tried to ignore the baby inside of me. Every time he would kick I would start to cry because whether I wanted to or not I was falling in love with my son more and more everyday. When you carry something inside of you for nine months you acquire such a strong bond. I don't even know how to explain it. My due date was January 11 and eight days later my doctor decided to induce me. I remember being transported to the hospital. I cried the whole way there because I was not ready to let my son go. I wished I could just stay pregnant forever so I would not have to be without him.

I checked into my room and they induced me that night, but this baby just did not want to come out. I had him January 19th at 12:45 p.m. He was such a beautiful baby. I only got to hold him for a couple of minutes after I had him.

I remember holding him close to me looking at him with tears rolling down my face. I told him, "Mommy loves you so much," and then they took him out of the room. That was the first and last time I saw him. This was one of the hardest things I have ever had to go through.

It was when I got back to jail that I fell on my knees and cried out to God begging him to take care of my sons. Michael is at a foster home while we wait to see if his daddy's mom would get him.

I know God will keep him safe and make sure he goes to the best possible family. I think of both of my sons everyday and wish I could be with them but I know they are safe and taken care of so that's good enough for me right now. I wish I could go back in time and change so many things, but I can't so I have to trust in God and move forward. Everything happens for a reason and God will never put us through anything we cannot handle.

I constantly say the *Psalm 23* to myself and that's what gets me through my hardest days. *"The LORD is my shepherd, I shall not be in want. He makes me lie down in green pastures, he leads me beside quiet waters, he restores my soul. He guides me in paths of righteousness for his name's sake. Even though I walk through the valley of the shadow of death, I will fear no evil, for you are with me; your rod and your staff, they comfort me. You prepare a table before me in the presence of my enemies. You anoint my head with oil; my cup overflows. Surely goodness and love will follow me all the days of my life, and I will dwell in the house of the LORD forever." (Psalm 23:1-6)*

18. FORGIVENESS — Eli Sandoval

I had a good childhood…at least until my folks got divorced when I was eight years old. Even after they split, the loving bond between both my parents and myself remained and they rarely allowed any tension between each other to be evident to me. I am sure it was very difficult for them to pretend all was well between them and I cannot thank them enough for their efforts.

I believe, deep down, I felt responsible for my parents' break -up. However I was not conscious of that for many years but, looking back, it explains a lot of the poor decisions I have made as well as most of the 'bad' habits I have become accustomed to over the course of my life.

Those 'bad' habits and decisions began with stealing cigarettes and smoking regularly by the age of nine followed by drinking as well shortly after that. The use of marijuana by the time I was ten or eleven led to weekly doses of LSD that continued, along with the rest, until my dear friend, Sean, never fully recovered from a 'trip' we took one summer evening at the age of 14. Unfortunately he was not the same person ever again. Since middle school, I have had repeated run-ins with the law, all of which have been misdemeanor offenses…until now. I am, currently an inmate at ACDF, awaiting a decision for reinstatement of I.S.P., a community corrections sentence, or a possible prison term. I have peace about the outcome because I have prayed for forgiveness as well as God's will over the future of my life.

I have been very angry with life, and the Lord due to the loss of my son at 14 months of age and two of my closest friends. Sean ended up committing suicide shortly after the death of my sweet baby boy and Ty, who lost his life in an alcohol related incident back

in July 1997...God rest their souls. It has taken many years for the Lord to teach me that as much forgiveness as we seek for our own sins from him, the least we can do is forgive others for the few times they have wronged us. *"Forgive us our sins, for we also forgive everyone who sins against us." (Luke 11:4a)*
I do not blame my parents for the decisions they have made, nor do I hold them responsible for problems in my own life over the years. Both of them have since been re-married and I am very grateful for their happiness and for the relationships I have with all of them as well as their love and continued support. I've realized that it's myself that I needed to forgive, not my parents. Parents need to support their kids all through life, it is so important. One day children will need to take care of their parents as well. However, life is what it is and it is as tough to be a parent as it is to be a kid and we all make mistakes. It's nobody's fault, it's a part of life. We love them and they love us despite our shortcomings, that's what 'family' is all about. Parents/children... they need our forgiveness as much as we need theirs just as we all need God to forgive us! That's how God teaches us to forgive others as well as ourselves and that matters most. *"Forgive us our debts, as we also have forgiven our debtors." (Matthew 6:12)* Thank you Jesus for His grace, mercy, and forgiveness!
Although the hurts and pains of life are more than tough to get through and it's even tougher to overcome the blame involved, there is a great peace God brings to our lives when we seek His healing and allow Him to renew our spirit while strengthening our hearts and minds. It's not easy to forgive and to let go of all the bitterness and resentment. But with the grace and mercy of the Lord, we are afforded the ability not only to survive desperate and lonely times but to become better witnesses for Christ and what He can and will do for us when the life He gave us seems too much to bear.

19. HIS STEPS — Robert Garcia
In September and October of 2010, I was charged with DUI's. I always thought of myself as a social drinker. The problem is, everyone that drinks in excess is fooled by the devil who makes us think that way. The law is specific on what your blood alcohol content should be, to be a legal driver. It doesn't matter what your

tolerance to alcohol is.

In 2001 my first wife was riding her bicycle at 7:00 p.m. Her purpose was to get some exercise in the early evening; she was hit and dragged 150 yards by a drunk driver. She was killed instantly. The biggest mistake I made is that I did not take this as a message from God to change my way of life.

In September and October of 2010, I was charged with DUIs. My court on both cases were pending. After deep depression had set in, my current wife and I decided to see my good friend, Robert, in Arizona. The second day we were there we saw the sights by riding motorcycles. After riding around for about three hours we started heading back toward my friends' home. As we were going down the highway, a drunk driver ran a stop sign and killed my friend in front of me with his truck. I had a skull fracture and 50% loss of vision in my left eye. My wife had minor scrapes. However, she had the task of attending to everyone laying on the ground in pools of blood. Two flight for life helicopters came, one for Robert and one for his niece who ended up having brain surgery. Robert died before making it to the hospital. My first wife and Robert's death were distinct messages from God for me to change my life.

After being involved in these tragedies, I vowed that I would not simply "control" my drinking, but rather that I would quit drinking completely. I would not let the devil have the opportunity to inflict his temptation in me to drink ever again. It has taken me a long time to get over Robert's death. I truly loved him like a brother. My first wife and I had already been divorced when the accident happened. It was heart-breaking to watch my two sons go through the mourning process.

After going through the tragedy, I had to face the judge on my charges back home. I received 60 days on my first offense and one year on my second, with no option of work release. In my youth I had two priors which justified the one year. I did a lot of soul searching while being in custody. I knew I had to change my ways and walk with God. *"The LORD is close to the brokenhearted and saves those who are crushed in spirit." (Psalm 34:18)*

It's easy to have remorse while in custody. There are no outside temptations to do otherwise. The real test is to serve God every day of our life. The seed of the Holy Spirit was planted in me at an early age. As I grew older, my direction in life was not that of religion. God has a plan for everyone. He uses problems to draw us closer to Him. We learn things about God when we suffer that we cannot learn any other way. I have developed a hunger for the Holy Spirit. My faith gets stronger every day. God has already blessed me by reversing the judge's decision and granting me work release. We have a minister in our pod with a master's degree in theology who leads us through Bible study every night. He is leaving us soon and has asked me to take his place. *"In his heart a man plans his course, but the LORD determines his steps." (Proverbs 16:9)*

20. SOUL SEARCHING — Dee Anderson

I have walked down many paths and traveled many roads most of the time feeling I was in this alone, but today I am here with God by my side to share my testimony. This is my story...seven kids, a mother, no father, no guidance, no love, no structure and no home. Drugs, violence, and abuse was the only normality we had in our lives. My mother was a heroin addict and she loved cocaine too, slamming it, snorting it, and in turn she ended up smoking crack too; she was a raging alcoholic as well.

It was scary enough to see her drinking or bumping a line, but it was terrifying seeing her tie off her arm and slam a load into her veins. I was just a child who's innocence had been taken because my mother needed her next fix. She never had the money so she would sell me to men in exchange for her drugs. I got molested and raped starting at the age of three. I constantly lived in fear. Somehow I always ended back up with my mother.

I was the head of the household pretty much. I was taking care of my three siblings and my mother (my other three siblings had not yet been born). I fed them, clothed them and found us places to stay. Sometimes it was just in an abandoned car, but it was better than on the street directly. I would just want to cry and close my eyes in hopes this would all go away but I knew it wouldn't. Sadly this was my reality.

One day my mother was in a rage and I knew it wouldn't be good; she told me to go get her the gallon of vodka off the table. I refused because I told her drinking was bad. She then got up in a rage, got it herself and said, "Why you got to make everything so difficult?" I told her I would never drink and I think she should quit drinking, so she pinned me down, knees on my chest, with all her weight on me, and one hand plugging my nose forcing me to open my mouth for air. She forced that gallon of vodka down my throat. I tried not to swallow but when I'd gasp for air, I swallowed. Then after it was gone, she hit me on the head with it, and cracked my head open.

I finally ended up in the hospital and child services got called. I got taken away and me and my siblings got separated. We ended up in foster homes, shelters and group homes. Somehow, we always ended up right back with our mother. The foster homes weren't any better. I continued to get abused and molested. Each time we ended up back with our mother, she became progressively worse. More abusive with the drugs and more abusive to us kids— me in particular. She abused me mentally, emotionally, sexually and physically. She would shatter glass bottles on my back, she even threw me down the stairs, burned me with her crack pipe, stabbed me, kicked me through a window, broke my leg and arm and foot and collar bone.

She would always tell me how worthless I was and how she wished I would die. Sometimes she would be involved while she let men molest me. She hated me as if I was ruining her life! I was only a child but she didn't care about anything she did or how it would affect me. Due to some things I've endured, I am scarred for life. She was going insane.

All this continued for years. Then one day my aunt decided she was going to take me, my sister and my twin brother and newborn baby sister in. She already had three kids and was a single mother. I thought this was going to be wonderful. When we met her, she seemed really, really nice like a mother should be. Her kids seemed real nice too! I thought surely this couldn't be true! Everything went well for a honeymoon period.

She took us to church; I learned about God. She got us new clothes, fed us and even read stories to us. She didn't drink or do drugs. She never yelled or abused me. It was wonderful until one day she found out she had to either take guardianship of us or her funding was gonna get cut short. So all this time it was about money! That's when the honeymoon period was over. She became abusive and she would even let her kids hit me. I took the fall for everything and for everyone. I was back to being miserable.

As time passed, I became more and more angry, bitter, and hateful. I started displaying it and was punished for it even worse. I got locked in a room in the basement; the floor was cement. I had no books, no bed, no food, no games, and no clothes. I was naked on a cement floor. This created more resentment. I started fighting and showing my anger. I ended up getting molested again and again.

I would pray but nothing changed. I ended up going back into foster care. I ran away and started gang banging at the young age of ten, but by age ten, I had the mentality of a 20 year old. I got jumped on by my O.G.'s and their sons and passed my initiation process to become accepted in. I used my anger and rage toward violent acts, making my way up in my gang very fast. I gained approval; they showed me they were proud of me. They rewarded me. I had a place to stay, I never went hungry and I was always protected.

I thought I finally had it made. Life was better than ever before. I still ended up in foster homes and group homes but my homies were always there. I bounced in and out of juvenile hall but whenever I got out I was always still protected, clothed, fed and housed.

By 12, I had gotten my tattoos for my gang: my marks in. I emptied my first clip at age 9 and by 12, I was doing big things. By 14, I had become a leader. I was respected, feared and powerful. I ran the trap house amongst many other things. Although I never got into the drugs, I sold them. I was robbing people, stealing cars, and doing drive by's. I had become the gang's youngest most powerful member because of my anger, hatred and resentment. I wasn't scared of anyone or anything. I'd go to any limit to get what I wanted. I was very violent and ruthless. I caught a federal case almost at the age of 14. I was under investigation by the F.B.I. and D.E.A. I got sent to C.Y.A. (California Youth Authorities) for almost a year. They confiscated 32 firearms, nearly $100,000 worth of drugs, money, a Lexus and a Cadillac.

I ended up burying 17 people at their funerals by the age of 15. I saw people get stabbed to death, shot, dragged by cars, and beaten to death. Even my very own cousins and uncles. At 16, I went to boot camp, got my G.E.D., passed with almost perfect scores, got emancipated at age 17 and started some college classes. I was still gangbanging and everything, but I wanted better things in my life. I decided I would enlist into the Army. I had to wait a while until I could ship out for basic and A.I.T. because I needed to get some tattoos removed, such as the ones on my neck and hands that represented my gang.

I began studying the Word of God and attending church, not frequently but on occasion. I liked studying the Word of God but I didn't prefer going to church. In my time before shipping off for the military, I did a lot of "soul searching," as you could call it.

I went and found my mother, she was out here in Denver, Colorado—in the meantime I still lived in Los Angeles, California. I came out here and knocked on her door. She answered high and drunk even after all these years, what a surprise! She took one glance at me and replied with, "Who the hell are you?" I was pretty disturbed by this and was tempted to turn around and walk away since she had no idea even who I was, instead I replied, "I'm your second oldest daughter." She looked at me in disbelief and reached out her arms to hug me. I gave her no response because I didn't know how, or what to respond with. She said, "What's the matter you ain't gonna hug your mommy? You know I love you. Mommy missed my little girl!" I told her I wasn't a little girl any more. I was 18, a grown adult and it was a little too late to be playing the mommy role now. I waited for her my whole life and she never came.

I just told her I came to let her know I forgive her, and I updated her on my life, my accomplishments, and successes. I asked her some questions and she gave me no answers and made excuses for what she had done.

I went back home to California. Soon after I went to South Carolina at Ft. Jackson also known as "relaxing Jackson." I completed my basic training, an 11 week program. I did my A.I.T. training as well in Ft. Jackson. That was a 42 week program. I completed that as well. Top of my class, top of my platoon and squadron.

I got a full-ride basketball scholarship to Sheridan College, so I decided to start attending college again. I played for two seasons and went back home to California on one of our off season breaks. Never expected what would come next. I ended up getting kidnapped with my twin brother. We got bound to chairs sitting, facing each other. Some members of the connect with the Mafioso and MS-13's had kidnapped us all because my mother owed thousands of dollars for all the drugs that she used.

They murdered my brother right in front of me. I tried to stop them but I was tied up so I could only do so much. They shot me in my knee, and stabbed me in my thigh above my knee, they shot me in my foot, and stabbed me in my arm. I was in agonizing pain and to top it off they murdered my twin brother right in front of me, his blood spattered on me. They left me to die with him. I was found by members of my click and taken to the Emergency Room. I had numerous surgeries. I lost my scholarship and got discharged from the Army.

My life was falling apart again. I prayed and God told me I needed to stay strong; that wasn't something I thought I could do. I endured so much I was exhausted. My mother never showed up to her own son's funeral. This was all her fault. I wanted to hate her but I soon found out she had H.I.V. and Hepatitis C from all the intravenous drug use.

I came from Los Angeles, California to Colorado once a month for a year to visit her and make sure she was doing okay. Sometimes she wouldn't even answer the door. She was so busy getting high. All I could do was pray for her. I ended up moving to Colorado because God called me to witness to my mother and try to continue to restore our relationship, or at least build one with her since we didn't have one to restore, so I did.

I ended up getting sick with spinal meningitis. I was told I had 24-48 hours to live. I prayed to God to let me die. I was so hurt and lonely and tired of suffering. I was ready to go because I was tired of fighting the battle everyday just to be able to live.

I had a spiritual awakening though: God told me I had a purpose on this earth and in this life. I suffered for over three months in Intensive Care Unit (ICU) fighting for my life. I ended up with a bleeding ulcer from all the drugs and medicine they were giving me, because it tore a hole in my stomach lining causing me to bleed internally. I was throwing up massive amounts of blood. I then had to get a blood transfusion from all the blood I had lost. I had to completely rehabilitate myself because I couldn't function. Meningitis destroys your brain and spinal cord so much it shuts down your nervous system, you can't walk, eat, talk or function. It was awful but I did it. I prayed and prayed that God would help me see through this and that He would give me strength to persevere and I did. God is an awesome God.

My grandmother then passed away on my 20th birthday from breast cancer. My mother didn't attend her funeral—her own mother's funeral! I dropped to my knees and asked God, "Why?" I continued to struggle and became depressed. I ended up getting betrayed and lost everything. I started questioning everything.

I caught another few serious charges in ACDF and bonded out in March 2011 but ended up back here in ACDF. I'm facing 10 to 16 years in prison but I started praying day and night again. God has spoken to me in many ways. I have found answers to questions I never dared to ask. I have found strength at my weakest times and happiness in the most miserable place. I finally figured out through God and many others like the chaplain, that God is using me to share my testimony to help others persevere, and become stronger in their faith. The most important lesson I've learned is to let go and trust God, through Him, all things are possible.

21. I LOVE YOU, LORD — Ella Lara Urbina

Since I was seven years old my life has been very weird. I used to have bad dreams, in them the devil would follow me trying to kill me. At the age of nine or ten I witnessed witchcraft being practiced by my family. I eventually became involved with all of it (sorcery, reading tarot cards, channeling spirits and consulting the dead). At the age of 13, I began drinking and using drugs. When I was 15, I had an abortion which really affected me and brought me down. I tried to find peace, power, and protection through idols and "white" witchcraft. I would never receive what I was expecting. At 19 years old, I got married to the wrong man. He was very abusive. I was severely beaten. I had my first-born child, Natalie in New Orleans. A few weeks after she was born, my husband beat me very badly, my uncle intervened and sent me back to my native country, Honduras.

After three months, my child began to get very sick. She was having a lot of problems with her kidneys. I became desperate. I returned to the United States hoping to earn enough money to get her better medical treatment. At this point I was deeply involved in my voodoo and witchcraft practices. I did not make a decision without consulting them first. Eventually, I brought my mother and Natalie to the United States. Natalie received surgery but she continued to be very sick and she was in and out of the hospitals regularly.

During this time I became involved with a big mafia group. One night I read a book called "Run Baby Run," by Nikki Cruz and asked Jesus into my heart. After this everything turned around. I started running from the mafia with my nanny and five children. I came to Denver and things were going great with me, my children and the Lord.

After sometime I was faced with a personal problem that really devastated me. Instead of running to the Lord Jesus for help, I began to use drugs. I caught a case and ended up in prison. While I was there I turned to the Lord and looked for answers. When I got out, He was helping me and blessing me. I walked with the Lord for almost three years.

Then one day I was told I was going to be deported. If I was deported my life would be endangered. I became fearful and ran from La Migra (ICE immigration). I was so confused and scared. At that point Natalie was in dialysis. I started drinking and smoking crack. I was lost again. I had became so depressed I had thought about letting the mafia kill me, because I could not go through with suicide on myself.

On October 30, 2008, I was arrested and I knew it was the end. I came to ACDF and did not contact my family. I was really depressed. Two days passed, I was called out to see Chaplain McDonald. She had a white paper in her hands with the devastating news. She told me that my daughter Natalie was in a coma. She let me call the hospital to talk to my family. She was in serious condition.

I went back into my cell and fell to my knees telling the Lord that I will not eat nor drink until she gets better. I began to pray, really deep. In my spirit, I brought Natalie in my hands with Satan at my right side to the throne of God. I stood in front of God telling

Him, "You gave me this baby and Satan that is my accuser is trying to take her from me." I gave her to God.

I was fasting and praying for days. In my spirit, I would go to her room and anoint her with oil, and put angels around her room. I was rebuking the spirit of death even though she was in the shadows of death. God put a lot of discernment in my heart. Jesus was calling Lazarus to come out? I used Natalie's name and called her out of the shadows of death. Then I went to *Isaiah 53*. I used some of the Scripture and prayed for her, some with *Ezekiel 37*. I did this for days. The Lord told me to put oil on myself as if I was Natalie, on my brain, lungs, heart, kidneys, arm and legs. I blew the spirit of life on those organs.

I soon bonded out and immigration picked me up and that was even harder. I thought they would give me a bond to go and see my daughter, but they didn't. While in immigration I missed my court date here in Adams County giving me a F.T.A.

My prayers and my heart were with my baby. They brought me back to ACDF. I asked the Lord, "What do you want me to do?" I started praying around the pod, anointing it with oil. I was loudly reciting Scriptures of the Bible while I was walking, fighting the battle of God for all of us. A couple weeks later we started a prayer circle and now the whole pod is praying together. God is moving in this place and is healing my daughter. She came out of the coma and is responding really well. "Thank you Lord, and bless all the girls in Pod 5. I love you, Lord. Amen."

22. THE TORNADO AND LESSONS — Julia Roberts

My tornado started as a child. I come from a family of ten. I have seven brothers and two sisters. Growing up for me was not easy. I was like the black sheep of the family. You may as well say that I wasn't born at all. I had no one to love me at all and no one to talk to out of all the brothers and sisters I had. I was all alone in this dark world. "My father," Lord only knows where he was.

My mother raised us by herself. The boys were her favorite. Lynn and I were the only girls. My mom gave her away when she was two and I was four. That hurt me so bad. I'm all alone, no one knows and no one cares. I went to school sometimes when my mom had the time to comb my hair and get me ready.

I was tired of hurting on the inside. At the age of 14, I ran away thinking it would be better for me to live by myself. I started out being raped, sleeping with everybody and anybody, just to have somewhere to stay. I met this guy and had my child at the age of 15. Trying to go to school and raise a baby was not easy at all.

My baby's dad used to beat me and make me have sex when I didn't want to. I felt dirty all the time, I couldn't get clean, I hated it. I was being raped almost every night. Wow! Another baby. It's a boy. This time I was around 17 years old. By the same guy, but he swore it was not his and started beating me again. I got tired of that too. So, here I am on my own.

I had another girl but she was stillborn. I asked God, "Why?" *"Happy are those who mourn for they shall be comforted." (Matthew 5:4) "And I know you can't heal a wound by saying it's not there." (Jeremiah 6:14)* I tried again to replace that hurt, but nothing could bring back that little girl I had lost. So, I started getting high. I got pregnant again with a boy. I really didn't want another baby because I couldn't take care of the two I had, so I gave him away to a family. They raised him to be a good young man.

Not knowing my son really hurts me. *"My people are destroyed from lack of knowledge." (Hosea 4:6)* I have seen my son two or three times. I was running from my pain, not knowing that God is really there. I was selling my body and doing drugs.

Things got rough, so I left and went to Texas and got raped in 1994. I have scars to remind me of everything I went through and I also have a baby girl. She is now 15. When I was carrying her I really didn't want her at all because she was a rape baby. I did everything I could to get rid of her but God said differently. *"Freely you have received freely give." (Matthew 10:8)*

By placing God first in my life, I realize that everything I have is a gift from Him. You realize that your life is not dependent on material things. It's dependent on God. I went through the storm with my own child. I couldn't stand to look at or have her around me. So, I gave her to the Wacon Methons Homes, she had a foster mother who took good care of her while I was locked up.

I got out of jail only to mess up again. I didn't want this child. I was raped. I felt shame and hurt having a baby. A baby from a rape is very hard to deal with because you think they are different, but they are not. I had to face my consequences no matter what. I had to *"Be still and know that I am God." (Psalm 46:10a)*

God's guidance and direction can take you anywhere you want to go. Just pray for God's perfect will for your life. So, if you think you are standing firm, you can be careful that you don't fall. *(1 Corinthians 10:12)*

I thank God everyday for my life and her's, too. I thank God for putting this child where she needs to be. I have love and understanding in my life, so I can see that she is really a blessing from above.

"Father God, I thank you for being my light and my salvation so whom shall I fear Father God? I will fear no evil, for you are with me. You lead me in a path of righteousness. You prepare a table before me in the presence of my enemies. For day and night your hands are heavy upon me; therefore let everyone who is godly pray to you while you may be found. Be still before the Lord and wait patiently for him, know that the Lord is good. Enter His gates with thanksgiving and His courts with praise. My heart is steadfast, oh God; I will sing and make music with all my soul. Amen."

My dear beloved child "Dominique,"

Dominique, I love you more than words could say. I want your heart to be made cheerful and strong. I know I have not been a mother or mom to you because of the way I had you. "Being raped is not a good thing."

"God gave me a blessing and that was you "Dominique." I love you and long for you. You are my joy and my crown. My love for you gets stronger everyday. I love you, little girl, with all my heart and soul. Please never forget that or think I don't. I love you. You are very special to me, but the Word of the Lord stands. Dominique, never pretend to be something you are not. The pain and suffering you and I are going through, I believe love is the purpose of God's command. Love comes from a good sense of what is right and wrong. It comes from faith that is honest and true. Jesus says, "I am with you always."

"I love you Dominique." There is a time for everything.

There is a time to tear and there is a time to mend. And there is a time to love someone that's very dear. Love, Mom

23. DISCOVERY OF MAXIMUM SAINTS — Mr. Leonard Dare from Set Free Correspondence Study
by Chaplain McDonald

In all the other *Maximum Saints* books I mentioned ACDF's amazing incarcerated saints, but in this book, I would like to mention an amazing former ACDF volunteer, Mr. Leonard Dare who just turned 97 years old this year.

Mr. Dare started "Set Free Prison Ministry Emmaus Correspondence Courses," which teaches approximately 2,000 inmates in three different states: Nebraska, Wyoming, and Colorado. That is phenomenal. The volunteers gather every week and help grade the papers in Lakewood, Colorado.

So, how did Mr. Dare get started this ministry? He didn't start with prison ministry at first. His sense of mission was to share the gospel and to find people who were serious about studying the Bible through Emmaus Bible Correspondence courses.

Mr. Dare and his wife Wilma went to flea markets, state and county fairs, National Western Stock Show, and to any place where they could set up a booth to display their literature and to attract a crowd. Along with the tracts they distributed was a card that offered to anyone who was interested a free Emmaus Bible Correspondence Course. He was persistent. At the State Fair in Pueblo one year, he distributed 65,000 gospel tracts within 10 days with the help of 16 young people. They received 84 requests for correspondence courses and delivered the first course, "Born to Win" to all of them personally.

A 12-year-old girl from Turkey Creek completed the first course and returned it, but when they delivered the second course she said her parents would not let her study it because they were of a different religion. Mr. Dare was disappointed and became convinced that the general public in America would not study Bible correspondence courses.

In October 1988, Mr. Dare was following a daily prayer guide from Emmaus Bible College. Listed on the guide was a prayer request from Phil Wagner of Riverside, California. He was requesting prayer for God to supply more directors who would distribute Bible correspondence courses to prisoners all over the United States. Several thousand prisoners and their families were already studying Phil Wagner's correspondence courses.

Mr. Dare was excited to find out more about this growing ministry. He called Phil and invited him to come to Colorado and present to seniors how they could help prisoners. Mr. Dare became the director for Colorado, Nebraska and Wyoming. Southwest Bible Chapel gave him a floor space where he could start the ministry. He and his friends started a non-profit organization, and in January 1989, they sent correspondence courses to 30 students that were transferred from California to correctional facilities in Colorado – and that was their humble beginning.

After retiring, Mr. Dare and his wife, Wilma, traveled in a motor home to promote the correspondence course work in jails and prisons in 1991 and 1992, to expand their ministry. They began visiting all the jails and prisons in the three states. They would take a couple of weeks and visit as many as they could, then they would rest for a while. Then, they would continue their mission and visit jails and prisons in other areas. This took about one and a half years. During those years, Mr. Dare and his wife also led Bible studies in the Denver area, using the Emmaus materials, and had good results.

Mr. and Mrs. Leonard Dare on their mission journey

Their persistence paid off. Their ministry, in 2011, Set Free has about 70 volunteers helping 1,500 inmates with the Emmaus Correspondence Bible Studies. Ninety-nine percent of the work is done by seniors. They process 350 to 400 exams returned by students every week. They give each student who completes all 72 courses with a passing grade of 70% or more a leather covered study Bible as a reward for their efforts. Once, Mr. Dare came out ACDF to give a Bible to an inmate who finished all the courses.

Mr. Dare shared that he never guessed that these correspondence courses would grew to this extent. In 2007, he stepped down from being a director to being an associate director. He was 95 years old. He firmly believes that the more students study, the less likely they are to return to prison. Guiding the incarcerated could reduce recidivism greatly because when people find purpose and direction in life, instead of striking back at society, they become functioning members of it: people who reach out to help others.

I had the privilege of visiting the Set Free ministry group at Southwest Bible Chapel in Lakewood. Mr. Dare asked me to share the Transformation Project Prison ministry. There were about 25 people working together and I was very impressed by their operation and the dedication of the volunteers.

They use a computerized grading system, and many people are involved in grading lessons. They add comments to the inmates on the lessons, which are graded and returned to them. Even if an inmate moves from one facility to another, they can pick up the study wherever they go. Their progress report is in the computer system. Set Free Ministry provides all the postage involved, and the study materials are free to both inmates and the families of the incarcerated.

I was touched by their generous heart. Their goal was helping inmates grow spiritually and mentoring them through the study. In the middle of the grading, they would stop and have a time of sharing reports, prayers, celebrating birthdays, and reading the testimonies of inmates. The day I visited, a man who had been just released from prison came and shared his testimony in tears and with heartfelt thanks to Set Free Prison Ministry volunteers. In the midst of despair and turmoil, he started Emmaus Correspondence courses while incarcerated, and through the study, he accepted Christ. His life had changed for the better. He had come to thank the Set Free Ministry volunteers who had helped him through the rough times. Set Free Prison Ministry volunteers were the unseen spiritual mentors that this man needed.

I thank God for Mr. Leonard Dare and the volunteers of Set Free. They are making a difference in many people's lives without going to prison. Praise God!

If you are incarcerated or family of the incarcerated and would like to study this correspondence course, you can write to: Set Free Prison Ministries, Inc. , P.O. Box 19760, Denver, CO 80219-9917. They will send you the first book, "Born To Win," and will provide the postage free envelopes for returning the study for grading and encouraging comments.

Wilma and Leonard Dare and Set Free Prison Ministry Volunteers grading session

Mr. Dare's wife, Wilma, passed away many years ago, and Mr. Dare passed away in 2011 in a car accident. He was 99 years old.

Part Two:
Sermons and Meditations

Drawing "A Guardian Angel" by Edger Perez

24. A MAN IN NEW MEXICO PRISON — Theodore P. Sanchez

One night at a bar, I was drinking heavily for about seven hours with the help of cocaine. That's when I ended up exploding. For all those years I had hidden my frustrations, fears, hatred, and anger deep down inside. I lost it and almost killed a man in what I thought was only a simple bar fight.

I was sentenced to three years in the New Mexico prison system, a very different and very violent prison compared to the Colorado prisons. You could just see the evil. Satan was lurking around every corner. Prison yards were shutting down because of all the killings: a combination of drugs and gangs. For the first year and a half I had never seen anything like it in my life. The guards were also getting killed or bulldogged to the point where the only solution was to record the entire prison population and watch and see who was who and what gang or group did every single one belong to, if any.

Well, when I had ended up back in prison, I had made up my mind I was going to seek God's kingdom. So I was known to be a Christian and talked to everyone. But I hung out with mostly my race, the Hispanics (not to mention—that's what one's required to do when in prison). Anyhow, I was sent to Las Cruces, New Mexico, a prison only designed to house all of the notorious gang members known to run all of the prisons: a gang called (SNM) Syndicate of New Mexico.

I was locked down 24 hours a day and only left my cell escorted by two or more guards, handcuffed and shackled with a lead shank placed on the cuffs—just like walking a dog, only to be placed in another cage with a shower in it. All of the inmates tormented me, yelling catcalls all day and all night, literally taking turns, shifting on and off like soldiers do in the Army, pounding on the walls, not letting me sleep.

During this hell, about two months later, I was lying there on my bunk listening to all the madness, and there was a knock. It was coming from below me. I listened carefully because now I could hear someone with a really thick Spanish accent using Spanish slang. (I thought I was starting to finally lose my mind.) But I came to find out it was the person below me. He asked me my name, and then he introduced himself as David. He asked my permission if we could start to talk to pass the time and to get to know each other. At first I was really cautious, because I thought he was trying to trick me to get information out of me; but I still went along. David advised me he was doing a life sentence for killing drug dealers execution-style. But now he was a Christian man who had been locked up for 20-plus years and claimed he wasn't a gang member.

As time went on, we got to know each other quite a bit. Most of the time, David taught me the Bible. We played a game where we would read a chapter, and at the end of the chapter David would explain it to me so I could better understand it. He would also suggest that I memorize a key verse every day. Every day he would pick a verse out of what we studied and turned it into a game, telling me that when he knocked, he wanted me to quote a certain verse. For example, *John 3:16* says, *"For God so loved the world that he gave his one and only Son, that whoever believes in him shall not perish but have eternal life."*

David said not to cheat! And yes, sometimes I did, and amazingly David would know, by how fast I answered the verse or how long it took, or just the way I worded it!

One day David called my name and said, "Theo (short for Theodore), soon you're going to be leaving Little Carnal (brother in Spanish), but I want to ask you something. Are you prejudiced? Are you sure? How do you feel about those miyas (Spanish slang for niggers)?" I told him, "I'm cool with everybody. Why?" He said, "Just asking." I had thought to myself, "That's kind of weird," but didn't think anything much. So David woke me up one day screaming and hollering, "Theo, pack it up; you're leaving. But before you leave, I want to see you face-to-face so I can give you a farewell gift." I'm thinking to myself, "Yes, I can finally put a face to this voice I've been talking to for almost a year through the vent." So I hurried up and packed and ran down the stairs to see the biggest, blackest man named David Watley. I was talking to a black man the whole time with a strong Spanish accent. So, I was really surprised. We both had crocodile tears and started crying. He said, "My name is David Watley." David gave me his Bible as a going-away gift. A Bible he walked those deadly prison grounds with for 20 years or more. A Bible I didn't use very much but still have to this day.

Now I realize how important it is not only to claim that I'm a Christian but also to be a Christian. Every morning when I wake up, my eyes focus on a picture of Christ Jesus. Below it, it says, "A life not lived for others is not worth living." It's a reminder of my constant objective to be faithful, fervent, and focused, first in my relationship with God and then in my relationships with others. To me, those three F's are vitally important. They help me balance my spiritual life with the reality of the world in which we live. They help me make choices every day about whether to honor and serve my Redeemer. They help me set my priorities in every area of my life—my family, my friends—so that I keep the Lord first. I am in the habit of turning to Christ Jesus every day, every moment, whether waking or sleeping.

Many of my Christian brothers' own transformations and experiences have helped shape my own spiritual journey, and I encourage you, brothers, to continue sharing your experiences in your walk and to share your prayer lives. Prayer gives us direct access to the power of God. People are healed and lives are changed. Prayer aligns us with God and gives us greater peace, joy, and fulfillment more than anything we could seek! We must live in a way that is pleasing to Him, for His righteousness also signifies His standards for human life. Led by His Spirit *(Romans 8:14)* and directed by His word *(2 Timothy 3:16)*, we seek to live in obedience to His will. May the Lord bless you all.

25. IS SUICIDE WORTH IT? — Lakiesha Vigil

I've been affected by suicide personally. I found my last roommate, hanging in our room. I've seen a lot of horrible things but never a person hanging two feet away from my pillow. I didn't know her too well considering I was with her only a week and she slept all day and night. All I knew was her name and she was a mother to three little girls, had a fiance, and also was a daughter, a granddaughter, and a sister. The day I found her in our room, I was shocked, frightened and angry. Why was I angry at her? Well, first and foremost suicide is a selfish act. She was only thinking about herself and not her children or family she was leaving behind, not worried how it would affect whoever would have found her if not me. Her actions affected me tremendously.

I have to take medication to help with my thoughts and memory. My room door being closed, light off, clothes hanging on the ladder, even blond haired girls were all triggers for me. I was afraid to walk in my room with the light off. I wasn't able to close my door or turn my light off during our time out. At first, I thought I could tough it out and stay in the same room, but I couldn't do it. I had to move out of that room. When I went to pick up my stuff, the clothes she used were still tied to the ladder. The image of her lifeless body replayed. I had to make sure that there were no clothes on the ladder after this. She had blond hair so every time I saw a blond head, I thought it was her. I hoped she was okay and alive. Wishful thinking!

One particular person I'd like to mention and thank for helping me get through this is Christine. I've known her a long time and lived with her before. That night I moved into her room. Oh, did I mention she is the only one who ran after me to help? Yes Christine had seen exactly what I did. We both frantically tried to untie her, hoping we could save her before the officers arrived. Christine and I helped each other get past the traumatic experience.

The meds helped ease the intensity of the memories. Of course I know nothing can erase our memories for good but meds do help. Christine respected my request, door wide open all the time, light bright and nothing on the ladder. She never complained. Instead she told me she understood and when I was ready to make changes, they would be made.

"Thank you very much Christine. I greatly appreciate your support and help getting through this and lots more. God bless you." It's been three months since D's death. I've progressed on my healing process. I don't have those triggers anymore. I shut my door now. Not every blond head reminds me of D. Fortunately I haven't had nightmares or bad dreams about it. Whether it's the meds or simply a blessing, I don't know. But, hey, I have no complaints. I am just fine without them.

Meds weren't my only help I couldn't have coped without my Heavenly Father. I believe "This too shall pass." Blunt, but super true. Only God can bring true healing. All you have to do is ask Him to help you. He already knows what you need. He just wants to hear it from your broken heart, out of your mouth. "Ask and you shall receive." Trust in Him. He will never let you down. The memories are here to stay, but through this experience I am hoping I can help one person to let go of a friend or loved one who committed suicide, or maybe even save his or her life from suicide by sharing my story.

Is suicide worth it? For many people suicide is the only way out, a permanent solution for a temporary problem; for these individuals nothing seems to go right. The stress is too much or the pain is unbearable. Rent money, car payments, losing a loved one, a bad break up. It becomes too much. "Do it, just kill yourself. Stop the hurt. Your are not worth it. They are better off without you." The voices never rest. Very often people believe these voices and end it all.

These voices are the enemy. We are God's children. We must resist Satan's lies. He will work overtime to bring us to rock bottom. On our way down, he will make us believe we are horrible people. "God will never forgive your mistakes. God doesn't love you." These are his lies. The truth is God doesn't stop loving you. You are the apple of His eye. He will forgive your every sin and He does not remember them.

If suicide is the answer to every problem life gives, I'd imagine the world's population would be zero. Everybody would commit suicide. We all have problems. One thing people fail to realize is the affect suicide has on family and friends. Even the people around you, people you don't know.

Losing a loved one is hard enough but losing to suicide is much harder. They wonder and ask, "Why? What if I could have saved him or her?" Suicide ends your pain and begins someone else's. So, if you are considering suicide, put all your pain, problems, and struggles aside and think for a minute about the pain and depression your family will endure. Ask yourself, "Is suicide worth it?" No problem in life is forever. Life may not be a piece of cake, but death is no sweeter. I was only a simple roommate but D's suicide traumatized me; now I am glad that God has helped me experience healing so I could write this.

"Dear D, well my friend, this is my good-bye letter. I was so angry with you for all this, but I've forgiven you. I really wish we would have talked more but the few times we did we had some laughs. I know the Lord has forgiven you. I pray God gives healing to your children and lets them know mommy is always by their side and loves them very much. I also pray He helps J as well. And whoever else was affected. We will miss you, never forget you, forever love you. Rest in peace friend. Try not to eat all the pop-tarts. Good-bye, always your friend/roommate."

26. SPIRITIUAL WORLD — Jesus Tovar

I was born in 1971 and, like most of us, my family was not wealthy by any means. I grew up in the biggest city in the world, Mexico City, 23 million people in the last census. My father and mother had to work full-time to provide only the necessities to survive in an over populated city. There was no time to do anything else but work, work, and work.

I grew up very lonely, insecure and afraid of everything and everyone. My father was never there to talk to me, to let me know he was there to protect me, and to love me. I accepted Jesus when I was twelve. It really did not make a big difference in my life at the time. I was 17 when we immigrated to the United States. My father was looking for a better lifestyle. As for me, I just wanted the company of anyone, even a stranger. If you smile at me, bingo, I'd call you my friend even if you abused me and lied to me, it was okay. I was an okay student at Fort Lupton High School. Eventually, I became part of the varsity team and even made it to state a couple of times. I even won some first places, but it was always the same way: my parents were never there. I remember always having to come up with a story about why my parents were never there.

After I graduated from high school I had to go back to Mexico to continue my education because I was not able to get a student loan. While attending the University of Mexico, I started selling books for a local book company. I worked my way up to general manager and eventually had my own bookstores in three different Mexican cities. I could buy brand new cars and fly twice a week. Not bad for a 25 year old man. I married a beautiful woman and had a beautiful house. But the damage was already done.

I was very insecure and had little or no self esteem. I started doing what a lonely and insecure man does: using my money to buy my friends. I was afraid of being alone, or maybe trying to compensate for the loneliness of my childhood. I started going to the strip clubs, and buying company, going at least 3 to 5 times a week. I needed to hear people say, "You're doing really good. You're successful. You're the best." What lies! You pay a prostitute, and she'll tell you anything you want to hear. You buy alcohol, drugs, and vacations for your friends. Eventually, I lost nearly everything, so I came back to the states.

But, hey! I was only 26 years old. If I did it once, I could do it again. After two years of hard work, I still had nothing. I needed to make more money to support the lifestyle that I was used to. I couldn't accept the fact I was a normal, hard working citizen. I needed to satisfy my big ego; I wanted people looking at me to know that I am the best. I cared about what people were going to say. So guess what: I found a way to support my old lifestyle! I started selling drugs. And here's where my real testimony starts.

At 28 years old, I was making seven to eight thousand dollars a month as a car salesman. But I needed to make more money because I needed to impress the prettiest ladies at the clubs. Of course, my wife was not included in all this and neither were my kids. So, she divorced me and married another man. That was just the beginning of the end. I was already seeing another woman. I did not care too much. At the beginning it was fun. I was making excellent money as a drug dealer. I started living the fast life again.

To be honest, I did not care for anything or anyone. It was all about me and my money! I started dealing with bigger amounts and more dangerous people. Some were smuggling hundreds and even thousands of pounds and kilos across the border. One day, I moved in with an individual who prided himself on being one of the most powerful "Santeros" in the city of Denver. Santero is a kind of black voodoo or African witchcraft. He had all kinds of witchcraft tools and gods in his house. Santeria believe they protect themselves by offering sacrifices to their gods which are demons.

Once you reach a certain level in Santeria you can talk to dead people (demons). They will help you and protect you as long as you keep on doing what they tell you to do. At the beginning, I kept thinking it was all in people's heads. So I went through an initiation process, and I have to admit that I still did not believe much. By this time my parents had became real followers of Jesus. I was told by the Santero Priest not to go to their house, to avoid a confrontation.

I went deeper in the drug world and in the practicing of Santeria. I remember the priest kept on telling me, "You have already crossed to the other side." But I did not see anything different. Then one day when I was at the house of my friends, I started hearing this voice telling me that there were black angels and white angels. Almost at the same time, I started seeing a black angel and a white angel battling in the TV screen. I was the only one who could see this and no one else.

My friends started thinking that I was crazy, so I stopped telling them. "What's going on? Why am I seeing these things and hearing these voices? Am I going crazy?" I told my friends I was not going crazy; it was the spiritual world. It was the dead people – demons talking to me, but why? Because, in a short period of time, I opened the door of that world. These occurrences became part of my daily life. I remember going to houses and hotels and everybody would be watching a "normal" program but not me. I was watching a totally different thing: creatures telling me what to do and how to do it. Sometimes I was high, sometimes I wasn't. It did not really matter.

They were always there. Why? What did they want? Did they really want to protect me? Of course, they did. You know why? I was being used as an instrument of destruction. I was destroying young girls and young boys, entire families, entire communities just to put an extra dollar in my pocket. I did not care if I was poisoning people; I did not care if entire families would not eat or pay rent because of the parents' addiction. I did not care about anyone but me, me and me. Was the devil happy with me? Of course, he was. My friends, drugs are weapons of mass destruction. Can't you see it? Young girls become prostitutes. Young guys become thieves. Parents get divorced. Kids grow up in disrupted families and eventually become like their parents. Jails are full of people like me. People who believe in the lies that power and money will buy you happiness and friends. It will not. You're going to find yourself alone, always looking for a true and honest friendship. But you're not going to find it in that world.

One day I visited my parents, although I was not supposed to. My mom and dad immediately felt something was wrong. They prayed for me right there in the middle of the stairwell. I truly believe I was freed from all those demons that I had thought were kind of my friends. I did not want to leave my parents' house because I felt so much peace, peace like I had not felt in a very long time. I left my parents' house and went back to the same lifestyle.

Everything was the same except for one thing. I wanted to stop selling drugs. Someone or something was telling me not to do that any more. I told my protector I wanted to leave him and the drug world. He became my enemy, and so did the demons. They wanted to destroy me. If I sold no more drugs, they wouldn't need me any more. The main reason why they wanted me dead was because they didn't want me to tell anyone about them and how to defeat them. I would keep hanging out with the same people. After a few months, I became a drug addict instead of a drug dealer. Now I can see from the other side of the street. The demons started harassing me more and more. They wanted me dead. I became an easy target. After all, that's all they really want: our destruction. I am not crazy, I can assure you. A lot of people are afraid to talk about these experiences, because science is one thing, but the spiritual world is another. If science cannot explain it, they'll call you crazy and put you in a mental institution. People all over the world are having more and more of these kind of experiences but are afraid to talk about them. Those voices that you hear are real. More real than this paper itself. When you feel that someone is watching you, someone is. You're not crazy. Demons are always watching you and talking to you; those who cannot see demons, they still hear the destructive voices of the devil in their minds. When you're drunk or high you can hear them more. In that state, you become an easy target, and they follow you, talk to you, especially if you don't have control of your senses. Nothing will stop them, nothing except for one thing: the power of the blood of the lamb. Do not let demons fool you, making you think that they do not exist. Oh yes, they do exist. I can assure you that if it weren't for the power of the blood of the lamb, I would be in a mental institution or even worse, dead.

After months of seeing shadows, hearing voices and watching demons, I came face to face with the devil himself. It was the real thing. I could have had a heart attack because of the impression. But the Almighty God had a different plan for me. I was not ready to die. I prayed to Him and went to my parents' house. I knew some mysterious force protected their house. Even demons would not follow me there. Right after my parents left, I played a Christian CD, worshiping Jesus, and after hours of crying and praying to Jesus, I finally felt free.

I threw away everything that corrupted me in the past. I also made a promise to God. Because I was able to see that the spiritual world is real, I said, "I finally know that you also exist, because you protected me from the hands of the devil. I will commit my life to you; I will spread the gospel to all creatures making you the center of my universe." When someone saves your life, you're forever in debt to that person, right? Well, Jesus Christ saved mine from the hands of Satan himself. Since the day Jesus came into my life, I've been having dreams almost every day. In these dreams, He is always taking me to a beautiful place. I have been in heaven. I am not able to explain this place properly, but now I know it does exist. In these dreams He has called me to the ministry. He wants me to be an evangelist. "Yes, of course, dear Jesus!" I replied. So, I am currently finishing what I owe to the justice system and in just a few more weeks, I am going to enroll in a local seminary to begin the process of becoming an evangelist.

Think about this man who died for you on the Cross. He died so you could be saved. He died so you and I would have hope. I can tell everybody now that I've found the friend I was looking for. I've found the friend I never had in my childhood. He is the only friend that would never lie to you, He'll always be there no matter what, to comfort you, to love you, and to protect you even if you are in jail, even if you are indigent or serving a long sentence. I can assure you He'll always be there for you, just waiting for you to say, "Dear, Jesus, I accept you as my Savior. I want you to come and live in my heart. I want to do what you say."

Next time you are in the middle of a drug deal, think about this: Am I being selfish for trying to put an extra dollar in my pocket? Am I living and delivering destruction? Am I being used by the devil to destroy people, families and entire communities? How many of these people are having to steal and prostitute themselves to buy my drugs? How many kids are not going to have food on their table because of their parents buying my drugs? How many little boys and little girls are going to end up in social services or government orphanages because their parents are buying and using my drugs? How many young boys and young girls will drop out of school because of getting high with my drugs? How many will commit suicide? How many will end up here in jail because of using my drugs? Do not let the devil use you with his lies of power and popularity. Do not let demons tell you what to do. They do exist and they're very sneaky. All they exist for is to lie, kill, and destroy. *(John 8:44, 1 Peter 5:5-11)* Do not let him destroy you and the beautiful people around you. Remember this, "Drugs are weapons of mass destruction." Instead of destroying, let us build the kingdom of God; instead of hating, let us love.

Let us start making a change. Let's stop drug dealing. One day you and I are going to be in God's presence and He will ask us; "How many people did you destroy when you were selling drugs?" He is going to make you responsible for each one of those lives, each one of them. I also ask you the same question, "How many have you destroyed?" Let's ask Jesus for forgiveness; He will forgive you. *(1 John 1:9)* We can all work together to defeat the devil. There's only one way to defeat the devil, and it's called "Love." If we could all love each other in the same way Jesus loves us, there would not be any more jails or prisons. There would not be any more crime or hate. I know it sounds like a beautiful dream but one day it will become a reality for a lot of us. I hope we all make it into that beautiful place that Jesus is preparing for us. *(John 14:1-4)* The ones that have repented and believe in Him. Those who not only believe, but practice His commands. *(Matthew 7:21)*

I know for a fact that a lot of you have stories like mine. Do not be afraid that people will think you're crazy because that's what Satan wants. All you have to do is call Jesus to come and protect you. He'll send a couple of warrior angels to battle those demons for you. They battle those demons every day. All you have to do is ask. *(1 Corinthians 2:9-10, Revelation 12:7-10, Mark 16:17)* The Holy Spirit will reveal all those things to you. *(1 Corinthians 2:14)* Come to Jesus and you will find the truth. *(2 Corinthians 4:3-4)* If you have questions about the spiritual world, either ask your chaplain or your pastor and he/she will   explain this to you. Jesus has defeated the devil and all we have to do is believe, believe in Him. *(John 14:1 -6, Ephesians 1:18, Revelation 12:11)*

27. ALL YOU NEED IS FAITH — Cassidy Watkins

I was clinically depressed for 16 years. I was waking up with the feeling of my insides tossed about, complete agony, and suffering so great that I was lost in complete and utter darkness. The devil sat by me constantly. I did not realize that God was still there, for I was blinded by evil and great torment.

The depression started when I was about nine or ten years old. I had been abused physically, mentally by my step-dad and also sexually by an ex-boyfriend of my mom's. My step-dad beat my spirit down severely and my pain only deepened when my mom never left him and is still with him to this day. She even justified the abuse, making it seem as though I deserved it. We were forced to tell my step-dad that we loved him and had to call him dad.

When I got older I rebelled, I called him by his name and no longer pretended to love him. It's because of this that I think my mother has turned on me even more and this day refuses to protect me. She lives in complete denial to the reality of what his actions did to me. I suffer from PTSD and was suffering from severe depression and panic attacks due to the abuse and the feeling of abandonment from my mother and real father.

I was taking prescription meds thinking they would save me. At the time I could not see that they were actually making me worse. I was constantly having suicidal thoughts. Every morning I would awake and dream of dying. I did not realize I was already dead and in hell because I did not accept that what I needed was God to save me and bring me back to life, a life with contentment.

When I was incarcerated, the Holy Spirit found me, (mercy). I began to pray, and I was enlightened to get off my anti-depressant medication. Weeks later, my suffering stopped completely. It was God's healing I needed all along. The balance I needed was from God, not chemicals.

I began to pray and found hope in what God can do; there are no limits. God is infinite (boundless). All I need is faith. God will grant what is good. I had a glimpse of the world of highest happiness (heaven) in a vision.

I would have never had my vision of heaven if I hadn't changed my wicked perceptions. I had vowed to always respect my parents even though they are not here for me. I also vowed not to ever inflict injury on myself or others, whether it be physical or mental pain. Thirdly, I let go of myself completely, knowing and truly believing that everything in this world is temporary.

In meditation on these beliefs one night, all of a sudden I could not feel my body and was at complete peace. I saw a small river in front of me, the sand of the river was like millions of small diamonds. The grains were of all different kinds of colors, flickering, and emitting colorful rays. The water was so beautiful and sparkled like nothing in this world. I could hear the water running peacefully.

I never, not even in my dreams, have been so soothed. I could not stop crying for I was so happy. The tears of joy would not cease. I could see flowers falling from the sky gracefully. Lotus flowers drifted upon the river, the river moving up and down very peacefully and slowly. I could see a golden path. The rest of the ground around it was made of many different colored lights coming from tiny specks, the specks being like neon diamonds. The ground was like looking through the clearest glass I've ever seen. I could see far down into this amazing beautiful ground.

I felt warm and cool breezes. Nothing mattered anymore. I was in so much joy that I had no thoughts of the world I left behind, or anyone, or anything in it. I could not see myself or my body, I was like a mist. Everything was bright with light that does not exist in this world. The light in that world comforts you and is not blinding. It's almost kind of cloudy, like a mist, tiny pieces of what looked like cotton from the cotton trees flowing freely in the air. This place was beyond euphoric in sight and sensation. There was a bright tree close to the river, with huge green leaves, shaped almost like hearts.

Then I came back to myself. I was still sitting on my bunk, in an extreme amount of tears. I could not believe where I had just come from and that it was real! My hands would not stop shaking. I was in so much happiness and shock. I will always do my best to do what is right because that place is well worth it. I can't even put into words how much it is worth. I had been praying every night for God to open my heart and mind. And He did. He opened my mind, body, and soul way more than I could have ever imagined. My vision as to opening my heart was so small compared to His.

I pray every night and then meditate in hopes of returning back to that land. I have no fear of death to this body. In fact I am now anticipating death in this life so that I can be born in the next. And to think there were times in my life that I thought God didn't exist. Wow! I was so wrong. All you need is faith and to let go of the old so that the new can come. Our spirits live forever.

I am so blessed to know what I now know. God showed such mercy on my once lost soul. I believe that anyone can go to heaven, just free yourself from yourself and believe in God! And don't let the devil ever punk (enslave) you. Always look at the reality of things including the reality of your own perceptions. Know that all the good we do will pay off! Heaven is real! Without pain, there cannot be happiness. A flower cannot exist without dirt. Without war I would have not known the value of peace. I believe in cause and effect. It is true what the Bible says, "Love your neighbors because when you hurt them in the end, it will come back on you and you are the one that suffers." Forgiveness and love are the most important things to attain for happiness. Being punished for doing right is more honorable than being punished for doing wrong.

Always thank the Lord. Don't forget what you have received. He highly appreciates your acknowledgement of His work. Appreciation of Him is key. This will bring you closer to Him. And know that He will return His appreciation for you. Don't ever think that He is ignoring your prayers. The prayers that go unanswered are the ones that in the end are not good or right or just have not come yet. Remember God knows best and will only grant what is good.

28. ARMOR OF GOD — Brandon Young

In everything you do, you must take our Lord Jesus Christ with you. He offers you protection from all things if only we trust in Him and believe in His words. Study the Lord Jesus and you will see the many wonders He has done. The greatest of all is His death on the cross for all of mankind. That alone should show us His commitment to saving us from destroying ourselves. We are offered a position with Him in eternity.

Two years ago before I came to Christ, I was out in the world running around with guns and bulletproof vests thinking that I would be safe because of these things. I was not. I was never safe. I wasn't a child of God. God was working in my life but I wasn't working for Him.

Now that I have come to God and given Him my life for His purpose, He has equipped me with the armor needed for His works. I don't need a gun to feel safe anymore because I have all the strength I need through our Lord Jesus. *"Finally, be strong in the Lord and in his mighty power." (Ephesians 6:10)* I now have armor far greater than any man-made protection. I have the armor that is given to all children of God. It is the armor of God. The devil is out to harm you, distract you, or turn you against God. God's armor protects all and is strengthened by His word. *"Put on the full armor of God so that you can take your stand against the devil's schemes." (Ephesians 6:11)*

We can't fight our battles without God. Out in the world if you have enemies you usually know who they are, and that is because you are living a worldly life. You can see them. But it becomes clearer when you begin to live for God. The ones you thought were enemies are nothing of a threat to what you can see once you give your life to God. You begin to fight His battles. You begin to fight against your old ways of life, even sometimes yourself, and most of God's battles you can't see, but yet you still must fight them because you now live for Him.

"For our struggle is not against flesh and blood, but against the rulers, against the authorities, against the powers of this dark world and against the spiritual forces of evil in the heavenly realms." (Ephesians 6:12)

We are not only children of God; we are His soldiers. We are sent across the world to do such great things. We are to overcome evil everywhere we set foot. We are to share our love and trust in God. To put on the armor and not fear anything evil we have to stand up for God against all that threatens good.

"Therefore put on the full armor of God, so that when the day of evil comes, you may be able to stand your ground, and after you have done everything, to stand." (Ephesians 6:13)

We need to be right with God, love God, and praise Him in everything that we do. We need to be an influence to all, Godly and ungodly people. Evil will flee at the sight of the righteous. Hold yourself and stand your ground. The ways of the Lord are peaceful and children of God are lovers of peace. *"Stand firm then, with the belt of truth buckled around your waist, with the breastplate of righteousness in place, and with your feet fitted with the readiness that comes from the gospel of peace." (Ephesians 6:14-15)*

God's word is the only power that can defeat evil. You are to arm yourselves with knowledge which may be gained from many places. But the only true knowledge is learned from our Lord Jesus Christ. With knowledge, you gain faith, and faith is what shields you from all evil. *"In addition to all this, take up the shield of faith, with which you can extinguish all the flaming arrows of the evil one." (Ephesians 6:16)*

You cannot only defend yourself. You also must attack evil. When you go into a situation and are not prepared for what that situation is to bring, you find nothing but trouble because you do not know how to react. That is why I feel you must study God's words and learn to be as Christ—like as possible. You cannot teach something you know nothing about. You are a messenger of God once you give your life to Him. You need to glorify Him. What you use and how you use it is your weapon given to you by God to protect and serve His kingdom. On the streets I had guns but my guns are no match for my new weapon. This one keeps me safer and doesn't harm my enemies. It helps them. My weapon of choice now in my daily battles is the sword of God. *"Take the helmet of salvation and the sword of the Spirit, which is the word of God." (Ephesians 6:17).*

You also need to communicate constantly with God through prayer. Through prayer you find truth and opportunity. It is your chance to speak to God and know Him better, the highest of all. He will give you missions for which you are to use the tools that he has given you. Fight evil at every chance you get. Prayer is a way to fight evil without hurting yourselves or others. It strengthens your bond with God. If you were a father to a child that did not speak to you, how would you feel? Don't you feel that God deserves prayer? We need to talk and communicate to our Father. It will strengthen you because you will create a stronger bond between the two of you. And with that strength, you will have the ability to let God's power flow through you onto others, who then will hopefully do the same.

"And pray in the Spirit on all occasions with all kinds of prayers and requests. With this in mind, be alert and always keep on

praying for all the saints. Pray also for me, that whenever I open my mouth, words may be given me so that I will fearlessly make known the mystery of the gospel, for which I am an ambassador in chains. Pray that I may declare it fearlessly, as I should." (Ephesians 6:18-20).

God loves us in all that we do. That is why He makes us strong. Our strengths are gifts from Him. When we use ourselves in ways to better the kingdom of God we are using what He has given to us and not wasting it. By doing so He will bless us forever! It is promised!

"I have set the LORD always before me. Because he is at my right hand, I will not be shaken." (Psalm 16:8) I pray that one day our lives will be so full of love and faith in God. Amen.

29. I PRAY FOR MERCY — Kristin Madril

By the age of six I had been influenced by people in the Pagan religion. I started cutting myself at age 13 and by the time I was 16, I had become a Satanist and was shooting heroin. I was extremely addicted, out of control, living on the streets, and into gangs.

In 1997, the day before Mother's Day, I was invited to a party at an abandoned house by a boy I used to be involved with. I was only 17 years old and didn't think anything of it because I thought I could trust my homies. When we walked in they handed me a drink already made and I drank it.

Shortly afterward my vision blurred and I fell to the ground. Eight guys began to rape me, one after the other. The next thing I remember is someone stomping my face and head in. Then I heard someone say, "I told you we would get her."

I remember praying to God and telling Him that I was sorry for whatever I had done. At this point, God was not a big part of my life. I felt that in just a matter of time I would be dead so I prayed and prayed for God to hear my cry. Within 24 hours of my brutal rape, I was rolled out onto Interstate 25. I was left for dead with my body all bloody and battered. I thank the Lord that a woman stopped for me and called 911. I was taken to North Suburban Hospital and put on life support. My mother was in shock when she received the phone call to come see me.

SERMONS & MEDITATIONS / 85

After a couple days on life support I woke up to my family crying and asking, "Who did this?" I was so angry and wanting to handle this myself that I didn't want to give an answer. When they explained the damage done to my body I could only thank God that I was still alive. They found numerous drugs in my system, including GHB, known as the date rape drug, which immobilized my body throughout my experience. They also found on my body: feces, urine, boot marks, blood and glass. Inside my body they found glass and semen. I was open from my rectum to my vagina.

Thank God again that the lady who found me and called 911 had copied the license plate number from the vehicle that rolled me out onto the highway. I then told who it was, but I was scared and didn't want to press charges.

Three weeks later I was able to see again and left the hospital with nothing but revenge on my mind. I heard that the guys were arrested but let go because they were minors. At this time my only thinking was God had other plans for them.

One year later, I found out that two of those guys committed suicide, and four of them were looking at prison time but were nowhere to be found. The last two got off the charges scott free.

Today I suffer from Post Traumatic Stress Disorder (PTSD) and hear voices telling me how dirty I am and I should hate myself. I have nightmares all of the time of me being raped or murdered. I take medications now because of this horrific experience I lived through.

On February 23, 2000, I overdosed. I mixed three different drugs at one time, which should have been enough to finish me off. My dad didn't know what to do because he was strung out too. He did call my sister and told her I was dying.

At this time I thought I was dead, already gone. All I could see was the darkness. I thought I was going to hell. It was dark, cold and empty. I had seen demons, and one had his hand held out for me to grab. As I was about to give him my hand, I heard the most calming and gentle man's voice. It was just beautiful, and all he said was, "Make your choice."

I pulled my hand back and turned around with my eyes closed. I put my arms out and said, "Please don't leave me." Everything went calm. My soul felt weird, but comforted. When all of this happened, my family brought in a priest to read the sacrament of the sick. I remember feeling mad at them but I was okay, God had me. After three weeks on life support, I woke up and started a brand new life with God. I had to relearn how to read and write.

I gave my life to God after this experience and my story was published in the book, *Maximum Saints Make No Little Plans* Page 40. I began my journey in forgiveness of myself and others. I learned that to be who you are is not a bad thing.

I am a strong woman today because I can speak out to others. I was able to forgive wholeheartedly by the power of Jesus Christ because I don't want to die knowing that I am in sin. I turned my life over to God, and with that comes forgiveness. So yes, I forgive all eight of those men and pray for mercy on their souls.

To those who have been hurt by others, to experience healing, start by accepting the fact that it happened. It's not your fault no matter what. I know some say it doesn't work, but my therapy helped me years later to come to grips with my rape.

I like *1 Corinthians 13:1-13* because I never thought I would be able to be loved after this or to love again, but this taught me that love is not judgmental or ugly, but beautiful, just like me. I am in recovery.

God helped me to be strong in faith knowing that He does have a plan for me. I know that it affected me in an awesome way. You would think that my hate and anger would overpower me, but in the end it is forgiveness that has risen above.

In 2010, I can say this, "Thank you Jesus for your love and forgiveness. God, have mercy on their souls, everyone makes mistakes. This takes a big burden off my back to be able to forgive. Amen."

Now, years later and eight surgeries later, I'm back to my bubbly old self. Forgiveness, ladies and gentlemen, there is nothing else like it.

"If I speak in the tongues of men and of angels, but have not love, I am only a resounding gong or a clanging cymbal. If I have the gift of prophecy and can fathom all mysteries and all knowledge, and if I have a faith that can move mountains, but have not love, I am nothing. If I give all I possess to the poor and surrender my body to the flames, but have not love, I gain nothing. Love is patient, love

is kind. It does not envy, it does not boast, it is not proud. It is not rude, it is not self-seeking, it is not easily angered, it keeps no record of wrongs. Love does not delight in evil but rejoices with the truth. It always protects, always trusts, always hopes, always perseveres. Love never fails. But where there are prophecies, they will cease; where there are tongues, they will be stilled; where there is knowledge, it will pass away. For we know in part and we prophesy in part, but when perfection comes, the imperfect disappears. When I was a child, I talked like a child, I thought like a child, I reasoned like a child. When I became a man, I put childish ways behind me. Now we see but a poor reflection as in a mirror; then we shall see face to face. Now I know in part; then I shall know fully, even as I am fully known. And now these three remain: faith, hope and love. But the greatest of these is love." (1 Corinthians 13:1-13)

30. GANGSTERS' SKIT — Donna Tabor, Vesta Hight and Lisa Newberry

This skit was played many times in D Module Pod 6 and also in the worship services and these ladies touched so many people. Three people are playing different roles:

(1) The Holy Spirit (H.S.) – Donna Tabor
(2) A Gangster (G) – Vesta Hight
(3) The devil (D) – Lisa Newberry

> H.S: She walks toward a gangster and shows her the Bible and says, "Hi, Jesus loves you, do you know him?"
> G: "Jesus? Who's that?"
> H.S: "Jesus died on the cross for you. He loves you" (She walks away from the gangster)
> D: (shouts at Gangster): "He didn't die for you. You aren't worth that. All you do is come to jail and prison."
> H.S.: "But it says right here. Jesus died for you. Ask and he will forgive your sins." (She points at the Bible)
> G: (She is listening)
> D: (says to Gangster) "Not your sins, you aren't worth the skin that you are in."
> H.S.: (Walked toward Gangster and said): "Satan comes to kill,

steal and destroy but the Lord comes to give you life abundantly. Come, walk with me."

G: (follows the Holy Spirit and starts singing):

"Jesus was a rebel...He was renegade outlaw, certified trouble maker, but he never sinned none. He lived his life by a separate set of rules the culture didn't approve so you know they had to bruise him. That's the way they did. They sweated him so gangster, everybody the same everybody does the same stuff, tattoo, piercing, smoking up, drinking, money and sex with extravagant living, man if this is the high life of puff, puff, pass that. You live in a vapor life from a casket. I guess I passed that. I'd rather be a rebellion and have a dollar in my pocket than a million."

31. POTTER'S HANDS — Julia Roberts

I never knew that life could be so unique when God has His hands around us. Jesus said, *"With man, this is impossible, but with God all things are possible. (Matthew 19:26)* I would like to thank God for my healing. How did He do it? God said, "You are safe with me. I am here to help you overcome the things that have happened to you." So, I started writing my story.

He told me to go down to the potter's house and I did. He took my old clay and broke it down and started reshaping it. I am a victim of rape, lost in sin, nowhere to run, nowhere to hide. "But God" was there helping me to become a new creation.

It was not an easy thing to do. I had to replay my life all over again. God said, "Just walk with me, follow my foot-print in the sand." He started rooting me from the inside out. He took away the feeling from being raped. He took away the feeling bad about men and myself. Then the Lord gave me a little girl. Then he took men and put them in front of me and said, "Come child, I am here."

From that day on, I am not scared of being around men. I thank God for saving me. Let God reshape you. If you do this, you will experience God's peace which is far more wonderful than the human mind can understand.

Healing comes from God if you move yourself out of the way and let God reshape you. You will feel lighter. Now, your attitudes and thoughts must all be constantly changing for the better.

So, this is a new beginning because God heals my heart so I don't hurt so much inside.

And I know that God is my best friend. He healed me: Amazing grace, how sweet the sound that saved a wretch like me; I once was lost, but now am found; was blind but now I see. *"Humble yourselves before the Lord, and he will lift you up."* *(James 4:10)* For I can never forget these awful years I have been through, but God granted me the serenity to accept the things I cannot change and the courage to change the things I can.

"Thank you Lord for walking in the sand with me. Create in me a pure heart, oh God, and renew a steadfast spirit within me. God restores my soul. He guides me in the paths of righteousness for His name's sake. Blessed by the potter's hand. Amen."

Jesus said, *"When Jesus spoke again to the people, he said, 'I am the light of the world. Whoever follows me will never walk in darkness, but will have the light of life.'"* *(John 8:12)* *"Then you will know the truth, and the truth will set you free."* *(John 8:32)*

What a wonderful God we have! He is the Father of our Lord, Jesus, the source of everything merciful, and the one who so wonderfully comforts and strengthens us in our hardships and trials. And why does He do this? So that when others are troubled needing our sympathy and encouragement, we can pass on to them the same help and comfort that God has given us.

"Dear God, help me set aside all the hassles and noise of the world to focus and listen just to you for the next few minutes. Help me get to know you and your purpose so I can better my life. Father help me live within today, seeking your will and living this day as you would have me. It is my prayer to have others see me as your child, not just in my words but, more importantly, in my actions. Thank you for your love, your grace, your perfect forgiveness. Thank you for all those you have placed in my life, for my prayers were answered. Your will be done, not mine. In your son's name I pray. Amen."

32. ANOINTED TOUCH — Mireya Vizcarra

Within a month or two of my arrest, I noticed people were helping Chaplain McDonald to edit *Maximum Saints* books. It had true stories, testimonies of how people have been finding God in the midst of darkness. At first, when I noticed other people helping the chaplain, I said to myself, "Not me!" I don't want to compromise my time, getting out of my comfort zone. I thought I was doing enough: reading the Bible, going to Bible studies, fasting for my spiritual growth and praying for my children. Chaplain McDonald gave me Prayer Project Brochures and they were a powerful tool and very helpful in my journey of spiritual growth. So, I was thinking God knew how much I was doing. Why would He want me to do more than that? Why should I do it? That was enough and that was my wrong thinking. God's word showed me differently. *"Then he said to his disciples, 'The harvest is plentiful but the workers are few.'" (Matthew 9:37)*

I was resisting and I was experiencing constant conviction because I knew a gentle voice was talking to me. I was being disobedient to God. I didn't have a choice but to follow what the Holy Spirit was pointing me to do.

The amazing part is: obeying God blesses us. We are blessed abundantly even more than we can ever imagine. My involvement helped me to understand the depths of other people's pain and suffering. Other people have been hurt in many different ways, as much as I was. If others and I were healed with God's love, everybody can be healed. This is the good news that He has commanded me to share. *"The Spirit of the Lord is on me, because he has anointed me to preach good news to the poor. He has sent me to proclaim freedom for the prisoners and recovery of sight for the blind, to release the oppressed, to proclaim the year of the Lord's favor." (Luke 4:18-19)*

Being a part of Transformation Project Prison Ministry (TPPM) wasn't my plan at all, but God's. *"You did not choose me, but I chose you and appointed you to go and bear fruit-- fruit that will last. Then the Father will give you whatever you ask in my name." (John 15:16)* I am excited to be a part of TPPM, knowing that my work will affect others in a positive way; it will help others spiritually. I personally believe that God's power has no limits. This is the reason I will not be surprised to see TPPM reaching out across the nation and even around the world. *Maximum Saints* stories have a greatly anointing touch and are encouraging. Reading them helped me to understand God's love and helped me to learn to love Him and

love others as well. *"Jesus replied: 'Love the Lord your God with all your heart and with all your soul and with all your mind.' This is the first and greatest commandment. And the second is like it: 'Love your neighbor as yourself.'" (Matthew 22:37-39)*
Now I understand why He created me and what I should be doing, and why I need to go through suffering in life. *"'We must go through many hardships to enter the kingdom of God,' they said." (Acts 14:22b)* I used to be running in life like I was in a race, but I didn't know where it started or where it will end. Now I know where I came from and where I am going – to my heavenly and eternal home. Praise and all glory to my king, my only God! Forever I will love you.

33. AFTER GOD'S HEART — Chaplain McDonald

There are many spiritual lessons God has been teaching me and I am blessed beyond measure. I thank God for calling me to prison ministry and that has been one of the blessings in my life. I LOVE MY PRISON MINISTRY, but that is not my first priority. God has been teaching me that my love for Jesus has to be my first priority. I used to think loving ministry is loving God. That was my misconception. The Scripture tells us to love the Lord with all our heart, mind, soul and strength, then love our neighbors. *(Matthew 22:37-39)* After God straightened out my priorities, my life has been changed for the better.

Everyday I am focused on building up my relationship with Jesus and how to worship Him. I decided that my life here on earth is for me to love Him. Also, I try to listen to the Holy Spirit so I will do what He wants me to do to make a positive contribution to God's kingdom. Sometimes I struggle because the Holy Spirit has different plans for my life and I don't quite see the big picture, but as I obey Him, I find spiritual freedom.

What am I learning from the Lord these days? The Lord has been speaking to me through the Scripture about David. It says, *"After removing Saul, he made David their king. He testified concerning him: 'I have found David son of Jesse a man after my own heart; he will do everything I want him to do.'" (Acts 13:22)*
This Scripture teaches me that if my heart is focused on understanding God's heart, I will be able to do what He wants me to

do. So, I try to listen to God in silence more these days so I can understand God's heart.

Prayer: "Dear Lord Jesus, help me to have wisdom and discernment to understand your heart. Help me to know your will for my life and change my heart so I can obey you. Lord Jesus, I love you and adore you. Holy Spirit, help me to be a woman after God's own heart so I can serve Jesus as I should. In Jesus' name I pray. Amen."

Part Three:
Extraordinary Stories of Former Prisoners

Drawing "Moses and the Burning Bush" by Rachel Marzullo

1. "NEW HOPE MINISTRIES" — Founder, Rev. Ray Chavez

Luther Chavez was a welder and he was hired to put metal bars on the windows at a juvenile detention center. One day, he was putting bars on each window including the window where his son, Raymond was. Ray watched him. Dad was outside working hard to provide for his family and Ray was inside with no intention of changing his behaviors. Luther had no intention of bailing his son out either. He believed that you pay the price when you commit crime. Luther grieved for his son's behavior and the punishment didn't change Ray's behavior.

At the age of nine, Ray was devastated and felt lost and indeed he was lost since his mother ran off with another man who worked for his father. His parents divorced and he never guessed or imagined that this would happen to his family. After that he began ditching school and was on the streets; he became involved in many criminal activities. He was in and out of the Juvenile Detention Center. He used alcohol and drugs to numb his pain and he had no motivation to change.

No one may have guessed that the boy who was sitting inside the jail and staring at his father would eventually become one of the most effective, spiritual leaders that built a ministry called New Hope Ministries in Lakewood, Colorado. His church is growing. In 2011, on Sunday morning worship service, approximately 1,200 attend church and 400-500 on Sunday evening and Wednesday night worship.

Pastor Ray Chavez is 61 years old. He and his wife Lola started a church in Denver in 1988, in his apartment. Two people attended. Now this ministry is reaching out to thousands of people. Pastor Ray has been in the ministry for 38 years and he and his wife are the senior pastors of New Hope Ministries. His goal for the ministry is the restoration of lives, fathers becoming real fathers and mothers to be real mothers, making Jesus real. He has seen countless people touched by God, delivered from addictions, alcohol, jails, prisons, and bondage. He mentioned that two heroin addicts delivered from addiction became pastors and began ministering to others.

This church is reaching out to so many people hurting from alcohol, drugs, gangs, jail, prisons, homelessness, and broken homes. Pastor Ray understands what these people need and how they can get help and be delivered from pain because he too had experienced what they are going through. Wanting to reach out to those who struggle with addiction, Pastor Ray started a drug rehabilitation center which now houses 50 men and 25 women.

A great spiritual leader and organizer, Pastor Ray's vision is big. His story is published and called, *An Ounce of Hope* and he distributes them freely in jails and prisons to reach out to many who are lost and desperately in need of healing and hope in Christ. New Hope Ministry is expanding their ministry. They have started a church in Juarez, New Mexico, and churches in Aurora and Thornton, Colorado. His vision is to build churches and ministries in several towns to reach out to many people.

NEW HOPE MINISTRY is located: 5303 W. Kentucky Ave, Lakewood, CO 80227. Website: www.cohco.org. Their drug rehabilitation is called, Center of Hope: and is a faith based non-profit organization. Jesus can change people's lives. Here is his powerful story of how God brought change in Ray's heart and also how he responded to his call to serve the Lord.

"FINDING HOPE IN CHRIST" by Pastor Ray Chavez
When my older brother Frank got into trouble with the law, he was facing prison sentences. During that time he found God and was freed from all charges. Frank used to take me to church when I was seven or eight years old. My mother came to know the Lord, but later backslid, and that's when she ran off with another man.

My parents were divorced when I was nine years old. It devastated us. We never thought that anything like that could happen to our home. Since then I was on the street. I found acceptance and related to others who were like me, coming from broken homes: Life of alcohol, drug addiction, neighborhood gangs, violence, and destruction.

My father was about 40 years old and he never married again. He didn't want other people to come and abuse his kids. He supported all of us. I was getting in trouble with the law since I was 14 or 15 years old, always in and out of jail. What was lacking in my life was Christ. Drugs and alcohol were my life and I kept using them until I lived with my brother Frank.

As a Catholic, we all believed in God, but the first time I met God was when I was 21 years old on a train from California to Colorado. I just got out of prison and I was on the way to my brother, Frank's home. He was a pastor in Brighton. The Lord revealed himself to me and I had a vision of my past. God's presence touched my life. God became real to me but I wasn't ready to give my life to Christ at the time.

In 1973, I had a homicide charge from a car accident. A man was killed. I was placed in Adams County Detention Facility (ACDF). The Lord appeared to me and spoke to me, "Ray, if you open the door of your heart, I can set you free." So, I did. That's when God started to change my life. Since then I was delivered from addiction; that was 38 years ago. I had no desire for any alcohol or drugs. If you open the doors of your heart, He will come in, and break the bondage, and deliver you from addiction, alcohol, and drugs. I stayed a week or two at ACDF and was released on bail. I fought this case, went to trial, appealed it, was found guilty, and they put me back in jail. Again I fought the case for the next two and a half years. Eventually, the Lord set me free. When I was 23 years old, I became a pastor. Frank passed away 13 years ago. My brother Joe never got involved with drugs, he went to a seminary to become a Catholic priest in his late 20's. Then later he became a pastor and went to work with my brother Frank.

Q: Any words to prisoners?

Jesus Christ was an inmate. He was arrested, put in a dungeon and sentenced to death, but his purpose was to set prisoners free. He loves them so much that if they call out to him there is not a wall or cell, prison, or law that can keep them away from Jesus. He can change a dope to hope. Jesus has paid the price, you just got to accept.

Q: Any words to families of the incarcerated?

Not to give up hope and faith in God. Keep believing in God, because He is a miraculous God. Never give up on incarcerated family members. Keep your faith in God. He can help them receive their miracles. Seek the Lord and you will find Him. Ask Him, He moves for you because he loves you. When I was incarcerated, my family never gave up on me. They prayed for me, encouraged me, visited me and kept believing in God.

Q: Any words to a person who struggles with addiction?
Addiction is a spiritual problem and Jesus Christ can set them free, if they turn to Him with all their heart, He will set them free.

Q: What steps must a person take when they struggle with addiction?
1. Make a commitment in their hearts and mind that the only way out is Jesus Christ.
2. They need to cry out to God.
3. Begin to read the Bible, attend church, begin to grow.
4. Never quit in ups and downs. God is able to change anyone that is willing to trust Him.

Q: Do you have any regrets in life?
I have regrets that I have taken a man's life in a car accident. I have hurt others; I should have never hurt them. I hurt others intentionally and unintentionally. I cannot erase those things but God takes our past, regrets and sins, and buries them. In the courtroom, I told the family, "I was sorry that this man's life was taken, I wish I could bring him back, but I can't." I wanted to let them know that I was sorry. Two weeks before the accident I was taking drugs; I was getting high. I saw a car coming on the wrong side of the road and I barely missed him. God told me, "You need to give your life to me," but I wasn't ready. Two weeks later, I was in a car accident. If we listen to God, we can prevent lots of grief and pain. Eventually, God healed me from all the hurt and pain.

Q: Have you ministered in prison since you were released?
One night God spoke to me to go to the Adams County Detention Facility and preach, but I had no desire to minister in jail. To be obedient, I went to the jail and asked a Sergeant if he needed anyone to preach. He said, "That's the last thing they want to hear." I left it at that, then a week later I got a phone call from a woman and she said, "A young man wants to talk to you." I visited him at

ACDF and ministered to him. He was saved and filled with the Holy Spirit. He was incarcerated for murder. He started telling everyone about Christ. ACDF gave me a room to preach, so I was able to preach in jail from 1982 to 1984. Then I quit going to jail to minister when I started revival meetings. In 1988, I met my wife Lola and the Lord called us to be pastors. In 1988 we started a church and we have been ministering for 24 years. Then later many people who came to my church said to me that I ministered to them when they were in prison.

Q: Any miracles that you have experienced that you cannot forget?
     One of the greatest things God showed me is God is able to use anyone. We were short $1200 to pay church bills. I said, "We've got to trust God." One Sunday morning, a young woman gave me an envelope. When I got home I gave it to my wife: there was $1200 in it. This lady was fighting a case of murder and she went to prison for life. She was the one who donated that money.

2. "ABC MINISTRY" — Founder, George Medley
     George, 45 years old, had been incarcerated numerous times. What he has done for the community since his conversion is phenomenal. He and his wife Irene own a business called Metal Movers. Two years ago, he started ABC Ministry, a non-profit, which supports a food pantry, a clothing bank and gives away a car every Saturday. They feed about 1,000 people a month.
     This is all happening at Metal Movers, in Denver, Colorado, the business he started. His business has 45 employees and over 6 million in sales annually. He leads a weekly Bible study at his business and 22 people attend. He also started a church and on Saturdays over 100 people attend the worship service each week. George's vision for the future is to start an orphanage and to help high risk teenagers.

ABC MINISTRY is located at Metal Movers Inc., their address is: 48 East 56th Avenue, Denver, CO 80216.
Website: www.metalmovers.net.

"40 Pages of My Mission Statement" by George Medley
I grew up in a predominately black neighborhood. When I was six years old, someone knocked on the door. It was Rev. Jackson and he asked my mother if he could take us children to church. My mother said it was fine. All of my siblings and myself started attending church and got saved on the altar. Even though I became a Christian, I was shop lifting and selling candy on the church bus. Once I got caught stealing crayons. My father sent me back to the store to return them.

My father was a truck driver. My parents loved us but they used alcohol and drugs. They had a bad marriage. They were always fighting and they abused us physically and verbally. I had three sisters. I was the only son. I got arrested when I was 11 or 12 years old for stealing a car. When I was in the 8th grade, I stole my dad's drugs and started selling with my friend. When my father caught me, he wanted half of the money from selling drugs so I gave him half. I stayed out of trouble for a while until I left home; I was 14 years old and in the 9th grade. I started smoking weed when I was 13 years old, using meth, cocaine, and then heroin at 16 years old. I got arrested again for stealing a car when I was 15 years old.

My parents got divorced and my younger sister ended up in an orphanage. My father and I moved to Texas, after which he went back to my mother to reconcile. When I went to live with them, they gave me $50, and told me to go back to west Texas. I stayed in town, started hanging around. I became homeless, and lived in a motel, a laundry mat, and a van. Sometimes when I was hungry, I went to a restaurant and after eating, I would run from the restaurant. I was able to work construction. As the building progressed, I was able to sleep inside the unfinished building.

I was married when I was 29 years old and my wife Irene was 25, however, she didn't know I was using drugs. The reason I came to Colorado was because I was a fugitive from New Mexico facing 30 years. Also, in Colorado, I was facing life in prison. I got bonded out of jail, and went on the run, ended up getting busted in Albuquerque, New Mexico.

God gave me a miracle and I didn't have to go to prison, instead I became a free man. Shortly after that I went back to my old lifestyle. It didn't take long and I got real bad and went back to jail for driving with no driver's license. I served six months in Arapahoe County Jail and six months in Adams County Detention Facility.

The best thing happened while incarcerated in Arapahoe county jail. I started reflecting and counting all the faces of all the people I had conflict with, 12 or 13 people over the last 24 hours. They were all punks. Then I thought to myself: "How can all those people be wrong." I didn't like what I was seeing in the mirror. A day or two later, someone asked, "Does anyone want to go to church?" Only one went, myself and the minister. The man who led the Bible study said, "Your problem is you never surrendered your life to God." That got me thinking.

I started reading the Bible and the words touched me: "Do not worry about tomorrow" and "Seek ye first God's kingdom." I questioned. How can I seek God's kingdom? I never worked for God. Then God gave me a vision like a television screen, convicting me of all the things I did wrong. I thought I needed to change. I cried out to God to forgive me. The Lord told me to lead the Bible study but I didn't know hardly anything about the Bible, still I tried to be obedient. The next thing I did was knock on all the cell doors and ask people to come out and join the Bible study. The first time, I had five or six people then it grew up to 20 people.

I was in jail but I didn't care where I was. I started serving God. That gave me a sense of purpose. I was in the elevator because Irene came to visit me. A man said, "You look happy. Are you high on something?"

I replied, "Yes, I am high on the Holy Spirit."

I made business plans so I could reach out to others. It was called ABC ministry. I wanted to create a business where I could help the poor. I didn't have to wait until I got out, the poor people were everywhere, especially in jail. I started giving away in jail with commissary by sharing with others who didn't have money. God has given me a gift of compassion, generosity and faith.

I wrote a 40 page mission statement which was a letter to Jesus. It was like, "Help me to quit talking foolishness," etc. My cellmate was 18 years old and I read the Bible to him. I stood up and read my 40 page mission statement and prayers along with Scriptures. I read it out loud everyday. Sometimes it took about two hours. That made an impact on my cell mate and me.

I started watching what I was saying since I was asking God to help me quit talking nonsense. Once I was cussing and God told me to quit cussing. So, I quit cussing but I was still cussing in my mind when I was upset. One day I had an urge to cuss in my mind and God knew it. Suddenly, I realized that God didn't want me to cuss in my mind, either. The Lord can read my mind and I had to clean up inside and outside. That was a new revelation to me. When nobody was looking, God was watching. Eventually I was able to stop cussing in my mind, and I realized I had to control my thought life. Be careful how you think. Your life is guided by your thoughts.

I decided that I shouldn't be using drugs anymore. I was in a mental hospital twice before. I was diagnosed as bi-polar, sociopathic and had been prescribed many different medications. I was using meth, cocaine, then heroin for 16 years. I didn't want to take the pills anymore. I said to myself, "You have been on street drugs all your life and you don't need any more drugs." When the medication cart showed up, I signed a refusal form. They were concerned and questioned me. Because of my explosive behavior, my nick-name was "Time Bomb." They thought I would be like a time bomb if I didn't take medication. I replied, "I want to clean up. I have been on street drugs and I don't want to do that anymore." I needed my mind renewed not medicated. I was able to handle a new life with no medication. Since I started serving God, I struggled thinking I wasted all my life for Satan's kingdom. I was struggling because I thought I had to be perfect in order to serve the Lord. But I learned that it was a lie from the devil trying to make me stop serving God and to discourage me by reminding me of my past sins. One day I shared this with a man and he said, "God is not finished, he can still use you." This man's words encouraged me.

After I was released, I had to chase my old friends away to stay clean. God changed my heart and my life. I used to live in sin and I was proud of it. But I hate sin now. Before I came to know God, I didn't care about people, but now I sincerely care about people. I went to the Heritage Christians Center (Potter's House now) and started to get involved in prison ministry for writing letters to prisoners. This man who encouraged me by telling me that God can still use me was the first man I wrote a letter of encouragement to.

I struggled with remorse and guilty feelings. I was sorry for what I did in the past. God had forgiven me but I had a difficult time letting my past go. I felt I was not good enough to serve the Lord. I have read, *Don't Judge My Future by My Past* by Dennis Leonard. That book encourages me and I don't have to live in the past, but live in the present and focus on serving God instead of being discouraged.

I promised to God that I would donate the first $1,000 I earned; it took a while. Finally, when I had the money, I gave it to the church to help others. My finances didn't get better right away. In fact, I went through hardships, but I said, "You take that devil, I am not quitting. I will keep giving. I am not giving up."

Before I finally gave myself to the Lord, I used to pray while doing dope, selling dope, and put drug money on the offering plate. I couldn't even get through the church service during the sermon. I had to go to the bathroom to snort cocaine. I couldn't wait to get through the worship service. I was selling drugs and was trying to feed the poor. This process didn't work. This time I quit smoking, drugs, and alcohol, and never used again.

God is sending people to work with me in the ministry. He provides all the resources and the Lord knows I cannot do this by myself. My wife is the anchor of my life. She walks by faith. She has really been an example of the heart of God, "Mercy."

The building I operate my business in didn't come easy. My background at the time wasn't established enough to prove I was credit worthy to rent the building. When I finally met the owners, they turned out to be Jewish. While the man was reading my application, I waited for 30 minutes. I told him that the man he was reading about in the paper was not me. I shared my testimony of how God changed my life. I had so much criminal background. I had no character references. So I asked him to call my pastor. The man called my pastor and he said, "I trust George with my building so you can trust him with your building." So, I got the building. God gave me Ephesians 3:20 and I am living it now. It says, *"Now to him who is able to do immeasurably more than all we ask or imagine, according to his power that is at work within us."*

God used Paul so God can use me. When I can I visit door to door and invite them to come to church. One day God was directing me to visit a house and they started attending our church and they brought the rest of their family. We need to develop an ear for God's voice then obey it.

I used to have a negative impact on others but now I can make a positive impact. I only have an 8th grade education, was in and out of jail, and didn't know the Lord. I used to say how I grew up in a crummy family. I cannot blame my parents. They didn't know the Lord. I used to hate them but I forgave them. I went through hell, but I realized that I needed God. "Thank you, God." I had to go through many hardships. I needed hope. I realized that I needed God. All we have to do is "surrender." God can use me to honor Him. The most important thing to me is winning souls. I used to be a hard working criminal but now I work hard for the Lord. A wise man wins souls.

Q: Any words to prisoners for encouragement?

You can use all your past mistakes and failures as stepping stones to realize that you need the Lord. Your past doesn't have to be your future. Don't waste your time on TV talk shows and playing cards. The key to having a successful life is to renew your mind with the Word of God. If you don't change your mind, you cannot change your life.

Q: Any words to families of the incarcerated?

Don't give up on them because God doesn't give up on them either. I had many people praying for me: my faithful wife, Irene, and my younger sister were praying for me. Many years ago, when I was visiting my sister, she said, "You are going to quit drugs and you are going to be a minister." She spoke a word of faith to me and at the time I thought she was "nuts." I didn't believe what she had said but it happened.

Q: Any words to people who struggle with addiction?

I used to pray and ask God while I was having a needle in my arm, "How long are you going to let me do this?" What I didn't realize at the time was that God is not going to do it for me. God wants us to exercise our freedom and we have to make the decision. Many times I overdosed. I finally realized that God wanted me to say "No" to temptations, to alcohol, and drugs. Temptation still comes but I say no to the world, sin, the devil, alcohol and drugs. Every time I said no, my faith grew stronger. God honors my obedience. The Scriptures says, *"and to knowledge, self-control; and to self-control, perseverance; and to perseverance, godliness."* *(2 Peter 1:6)* God's Word is sowing and reaping what you sow, and you will reap good or bad.

Q: What steps must a person take when they struggle with addiction?
(1) Turn your life to Christ.
(2) Have reverence toward God.
(3) Renew your mind by reading the Bible.
(4) Change your companions.
(5) Act what you have learned from the Bible. What you sow is what you reap. *Mark 4:24* says, *"'Consider carefully what you hear,' he continued. 'With the measure you use, it will be measured to you — and even more.'"*

Q: What are your regrets in life?
     I wasted so much time in the past and I feel badly for all the people I have hurt. God forgave me my sins and I am thankful. I regret that I did not surrender sooner. I should have done this sooner.

3. THE ORGANIZER OF "ABC MINISTRY" — Irene Chavez
     Irene is George Medley's wife. She has never struggled with addiction of alcohol, drugs or been incarcerated. But she endured greatly when her husband, George, suffered from addiction and was in and out of jails and prisons.
     I believe every successful story behind any prisoner is someone who believed in them. Some families abandon their loved ones, but some continue to believe in them and have hope that they will change someday. They support their family member no matter what happens. Many families of prisoners suffer when their family members are incarcerated. Many times they feel helpless about watching their loved ones destroy themselves by addiction or destructive behaviors. This is what Irene felt but she continued to

pray for him and give him support. His successful transition and leadership is the result of God's grace and his wife, Irene's faith and love. Here is her story.

"NO REGRETS," by Irene Chavez

I am 42 years old and I grew up in a loving family. My mother, Maria, was my best friend and taught me to be a peace maker. My step dad, Peter, taught me to have respect for others. He was in the military and we traveled a lot. I had faith in God since I was little. My mother told me Jesus was real. When I had nightmares, she told me to ask Jesus for help. I had some spiritual experiences that I will never forget. There was a room in my house that I was scared to go into. One day I closed my eyes and prayed, "Jesus, I don't want to be here." Two times, when I opened my eyes, I was transported to a different level of the house. God was so real to me. I finished college with a Bachelor's degree in marketing and graphic design and became a commercial artist.

While living in Albuquerque, New Mexico, I met a man named, "David" at a party through a friend. I dated him for a couple of years. He had property and was selling cars. We got married and there were lots of things I didn't know about him. I kept my last name since I was an artist and as I look back it was a good thing since David had many secrets. He was wanted in two different states and was using different names.

The first time I found out that he was using an alias, was when my step son, Josh, came to visit, he said, "My father has two names." When my husband came home, I asked, "Do you have two names?" He denied it and said, "You know how kids make up stories." I believed him.

I had no clue that George had been on drugs for a long time. He was real good at covering up. I've never been around people who used drugs, so I was blinded to think that since he was drinking a lot, he was just sick. But his behaviors got worse and worse.

One day I was stunned when I saw stacks of money on the desk. Another time I opened the refrigerators in the garage and I was surprised to see blocks of marijuana. I saw a big car that was filled with marijuana. I know now why all the cabinets in the garage had locks. I wondered what was inside of it.

Three years after I got married, the police raided my mother's home and my husband was arrested. But this time the police told us his name was not David but George. He was in and out of jail a lot since then. I got phone calls from family members telling me George was being chased by the police and the helicopter, which was shown on the news. He was wanted by the FBI. I had no idea what was happening to him. I was getting upset, anxious, and feeling confused when local police arrested me because I was George's wife. They thought I was doing something wrong just because I was with George. I was devastated and traumatized. I was living in shock and fear. I lived as if I was holding my breath all the time.

George was constantly getting into trouble. Everything was happening so fast and I didn't know how to help him. Plus he had anger problems. One day he got into fights with 11 people, either shouting back and forth or fist fighting, in one hour. I tried to calm him, but I wasn't able to. He got kicked out of places because he was bullying people or he didn't like the way they looked at him. He didn't care about anything. He was drinking all the time. He didn't consider anyone else's feelings, as if he had no conscience. Later he told me he was doing heavy drugs until 2004, but all that time I thought he was just drunk. I had no idea he was doing drugs. Sometimes I smelled something but he told me it was chemicals from working on a car.

Sometimes he was up for 6 days then slept 7 days. I woke him up twice a day, gave him food and he went back to sleep. I felt he was committing suicide little by little. One day his whole body was yellow. I took him to urgent care but they were closed. I took him to a motel to take care of him. I wanted him to pass out so I could take care of him. He kept insisting that we should leave the motel.

I kept telling him I needed to go to the restroom. I remember praying, "Lord, please make him pass out so he can stay here, so he wouldn't get into trouble." I had gone to the bathroom five times. He wasn't thinking clearly, he didn't even realize that I went to the restroom so many times. He finally passed out. I took care of him. I had to sell the cars to pay the rent.

I was in turmoil when I sensed that he was using some kind

of heavy drugs because of his massive mood swings. I didn't know how to help him. All I could think to do was pray. I lived like this for 12 years. We were in and out of motels, pop up camper, cooking and trying to take care of him. I thought he was sick. Nobody wants to leave when someone is sick. I thought he would die or he would kill himself by overdose or kill somebody else. It was like being in a constant state of shock.

One time I was so upset I was going to leave him. My mother said, "If you leave him in the worst time of his life, you will never forgive yourself." So, I prayed, "Lord, I will stay and help him. When he is healed, then I will leave him."

George was again arrested. When he got out of jail, I went to pick him up but I couldn't find him. Later, I learned that he walked to the bar. The police arrested him again for fighting in the bar. This happened while his son was with us. The police raided my home so many times. There were times he was arrested four times in one month.

Another time he went on a drive with our dog, Grizzley and came back without him. He didn't even realize that he took our dog. I loved Grizzley and I had to go and find him.

I've learned that a drug addict and alcoholic lies constantly. He lied about where he was. He would be gone for a little while, he was gone for two days to two weeks. I was in agony and worried about him, but when he came back, I felt relieved. I never locked him out of the house, so he could always come home. I was glad he was not living in the alleys and was alive when he came back. I fixed meals for him.

When this pattern persisted, I prayed, "Lord don't let him treat me like this anymore. I hated being alone." My mother would move in many times to comfort me. He was gone so much and so many times I would get a phone call from a jail and George said, "You got to come and bail me out." He was so messed up.

One day I was crying and praying. Then I felt someone was in the room and I saw a big face in the room, a part of eyes and nose. I believe God literally appeared to me to comfort me. After that I didn't feel alone any more.

George's sister gave me advice. She said, "You have to claim things." I started praying. "Lord, this is beneficial for you, for

George and me. Thank you for making George just like you, Jesus."
At that time I didn't believe it and I was crying, but I kept repeating
it out loud. Faith comes by hearing but at the same time I could hear
a negative voice, "That's the biggest lie you are saying." Then I
would say it out loud, "Thank you for making George like you." I
kept proclaiming it. I didn't see the vision for the future but my
sister-in-law's words encouraged me.

I read Scriptures to George, prayed for him, and played
Christian music when he was in the car. He hated it and turned it off.
I would lay my hand over his head when he was sleeping and prayed
over him without touching his head. I kept praying for his healing.

We lived in Colorado about nine years. Every time I was at
the breaking point and couldn't handle it or breathe, he went to jail.
That was a break for me as if God knew I needed a break.

At that time I felt so exhausted. I weighed 98 pounds with all
the worries and stress I had to endure until I was 36 years old. All
the police raids and I was worrying that he was driving. He didn't
have a driver's license plus he was always arguing, and obnoxious.
He was not in his right mind. He would wake me up when I slept,
just to tell me to scoot over. During twelve years of panic every day
was the same, passing my birthday, never celebrated an anniversary.

In 2005 the last time he went to jail, I went to visit him.
And it was the first time he asked me, "How are you doing?" This
was the first time I noticed that he was changed. After he was
released, he said he was saving $1,000 to give to God and he did. He
said he was going to serve God. I didn't believe it at first because he
had lied to me so many times. He didn't like the way he was living
and wanted to change.

So, I thought to myself I will give him six months to make
sure he had changed, to make sure he was going to be okay and live.
I waited a few months and one day he said, "I am going to go to the
store and I will be back." Anytime he said that to me before, he lied
to me and went to find drugs.

This time he didn't disappear. I was finally convinced that
he was healed. He started watching praise and worship service on
TV and reading the Bible. I was so drained at that point though. I
was grateful to God that George was not going to die.

George said, "I can take care of things now."

I said, "You never apologized for how you treated me for all these years."

He said, "Well, I'm sorry."

I said, "That doesn't cut it."

George asked, "Don't you love me any more?"

"After all these years I find it hard to like you but I don't want you to die."

He said he could handle everything. I felt like my job was finished. I don't have to be around him anymore since I told the Lord when he was healed, I would leave him. Just before I walked out, I knew in my mind, I was never coming back. I was comforted by that thought. When I was in the truck, I heard a man's voice twice telling me, "George is not your enemy." I knew that came from the Lord. All of a sudden I had a revelation. George isn't my enemy. The devil was the enemy. George was used by the devil for so long. The Lord had to speak to me to change my mind.

I went back inside and I told him about the voice I heard and said, "Everything is going to be alright."

It took almost a year until I could finally believe that he was a changed man. But for so long, I suffered from bad memories and I had to change my way of thinking as well. When he was doing drugs, he would talk softly. After George changed, he talked softly. That reminded me of when he was on drugs. I was on alert all the time to discern if what he was doing was truly changed behavior or not.

I learned to say, "Satan get behind me. He is a changed man of God."

After that I was able to trust him. I had to tell myself literally. I need to submit to him. That is the hardest thing that I ever had to learn. I had to heal from fear and relearn how to live.

Still, if someone would have told me about what we would be doing for the Lord in later years, I would have never believed it. God was merciful to me. He helped me to forgive and have compassion for my husband.

My name, "Irene" means peaceful. It seems as though God surrounded me with a protective bubble. He gave me the wisdom to know that George was sick. I learned not to get angry with little things. You learn to pick your battles. No one is going to be loving all the time. God gives us examples of love in the Scripture: *"Love is patient, love is kind. It does not envy, it does not boast, it is not proud. It is not rude, it is not self-seeking, it is not easily angered, it keeps no record of wrongs. Love does not delight in evil but rejoices with the truth. It always protects, always trusts, always hopes, always perseveres. Love never fails."* (1 Corinthians 13:4-8a)

God loved George and showed His love through me. The Lord also gave me the ability to endure. George didn't like people and couldn't stand being around them. Now he loves people. Only God can do that, change a man's heart. He went from a hater of people to a lover of people.

Q: Any words to prisoners for encouragement?

This is the shortest time we have compared to eternity. This life is where we prove ourselves. Do we want to honor God for eternity or are we too stubborn to do things His way? Our enemy tries to force us to look down and that is a waste of time. I pray, "I am not only grateful that you love us, but that you made yourself known to us. You could have existed and not even made yourself known."

Q: Any words to families of the incarcerated?

You cannot blame someone who doesn't know better. You cannot blame a man who is blind, that they cannot see. That may be your incarcerated family member's case. Continue praying for them and stand in the gap – constant prayer, and encouragement to the prisoners will help them. Rely on God, so you can get through it with His help. God helped me to get through it. Remember that no matter how bad I thought I had been treated or how rough it had been for me, I always knew George had it worse. He hated himself and hated his life. So, have mercy on your family member who struggles from addiction.

Q: Any words to people who struggle with addiction?

Hold every thought captive and compare it to the will of God. The only way of knowing that is to know the Bible. Read the Word that is alive and talk to God. George never stumbled after God changed him, and I am talking about someone who loved sin, but he never went back to his old ways.

Q: What steps must a person take when they struggle with addiction?
(1) Submit to God.
(2) Repent.
(3) Devote time to Him, read the Bible, talk to Him, wait on Him, wait for an answer.
(4) Change your circle of influences, friends, and find a church where you can grow spiritually.
(5) Don't go back to your familiar environment but focus on Jesus.

Q: Any miracles that you have experienced that you cannot forget?
George is a miracle to me. He had no conscience and cared about nothing but now he cares about everything. He cares about God more than anything, and he cares about God's people. George is a man after God's heart. He is not ashamed of the gospel. If someone is upset while waiting in the grocery line, he will talk to others about God while waiting. His whole life is focused on spreading the gospel of Jesus. Without the Lord, he told me he didn't have a reason to get out of the bed. His purpose has to be living for the Lord and George is living it now.

Q: What are your regrets in life?
If I changed anything, the outcome would be different. I don't know if I would change anything. George and I both needed to grow. I was really naive and I had to be strong for my husband. I am amazed with what God has done with us, serving God together. George is a servant of God and I stand by him. I couldn't have asked for anything more. If you asked me that question ten years ago, I would have had a lot of answers for you. Lots of regrets at the time but God didn't show me the end result. If He had, I would have had more hope, then it really wouldn't be a true molding of my character. God doesn't give us the whole picture of our lives.

Q: How are you involved in ministry?
George is the visionary and he sees the finished products. He

gives me directions on what I should do to help him to accomplish it. I organize the food bank. I purchase food and oversee what needs to be done to make things go smooth. We have many volunteers: my Aunt Julia, Arlene, and about five others including a USF Trucking Company which picks up the food and delivers for us. When people donate cars, the profit goes to the food bank. We are serving about 1,000 people every month. We give two big bags of groceries to each person who comes to the food bank.

4. "OPEN DOOR, YOUTH GANG ALTERNATIVES"
Founder Rev. Leon Kelly

Reverend Leon Kelly is 58 years young and serves as the Executive Director of Open Door Youth Gang Alternatives. He is the founder and driving force behind this ministry. Open Door is the oldest anti-gang program still in existence in the Denver metro area, a one-of-a-kind agency that was founded in December, 1987. It is a non-profit, non-law enforcement agency with the sole mission of curbing gang recruitment, and reducing street gang violence. Open Door Youth Gang Alternatives reaches kids through a variety of activities that include in-school and after-school programs, parenting classes, employment and job training for teens, family and victim support, gang mediation and intervention, public education and community awareness. Rev. Kelly began his ministry 28 years ago when he noticed changes occurring within Denver, including a huge influx of gangs from California. He experienced difficult times as a young man himself. He served three years in a Colorado penitentiary on a 5-8 year sentence.

One of the components of his ministry is an after-school program in one of Denver's schools. The after-school program serves approximately 180-200 children ages 6-14. It provides academic support as well as character education with a strong emphasis on self-discipline and self-improvement, all in an effort to help the children make positive choices when confronted by negative influences.

Rev. Kelly's work is crucial because America has the largest prison population in the world. Many children are growing up without parents, especially fathers. Many children who joined gangs had moms who cared for them but most of them grew up without a dad figure in their lives.

Without a dad figure in a child's life, there is something missing—security and protection and nurturing etc. Unless someone can fill that gap, these children may be searching for a father figure in the wrong place like in the streets and through gang affiliation. That's what Rev. Kelly tries to prevent. He became a father to many children. He is trying to save children from gangs, prison, and early violent death.

When Rev. Kelly saw the need, he acted on it. Open Door Youth Gang Alternatives has been reaching out to many who choose to walk the right path. He is educating the public and children about the dangers of being involved in gangs and how to avoid the destructive path of addiction, gangs, and prison. He continues to be a positive role model for many people in the community and brings transformation to many by reaching out to young children.

In Rev. Kelly's office, he has a list of the young people who have died a violent death in the Denver metro area. As of June 18, 2011, there had been 996 since he started ministry. Many of them he knew. One of the records Rev. Kelly holds is that he has buried more young people in the State than any other minister, sometimes burying two or three young people in a week. It is not a record that he is proud of, but through these deaths he has had the privilege of supporting the families as they go through these difficult times. The list on the wall reminds him that there is still plenty of work to do. It motivates him to continue his work.

In 2010, Rev. Kelly received a pardon from the Colorado Governor. His tireless work for kids and the community have been recognized by many people and organizations. Receiving a pardon was something that Rev. Kelly is proud of. He certainly deserves it. We don't have any idea how many children are saved from dying violent deaths and gang related criminal activities because of his efforts. I believe there will be many more people who are touched by his ministry.

OPEN DOOR YOUTH GANG ALTERNATIVES is located at 1615 California #712, Denver, Colorado, 80202, 303-893-GANG (4264). Website: www.therev.org. Open Door is a non-profit, community based, non-law enforcement organization.

"MY STORY" by Rev. Leon Kelly

I am a PK (preacher's kid); my grandfather and father were ministers. My mother was a preacher's wife and missionary, and she had the highest position in the church as a woman. My parents had six children, three sons and three daughters. I am the first-born male and my dad taught me about hard work and instilled the importance of a strong work ethic in my life. My father was a pillar in the community. I didn't want to be a pastor because of what I saw him go through. Although I was not interested in ministry, I still attended church three or four times a week and all day on Sunday. Faith and my relationship with God was always a big part of my life. I played basketball and football at East High School in Denver and headed to University of Colorado (CU) for college.

When I left home and started attending CU in Boulder, I was exposed to a new world. The hedge that had been built around me was no longer there. I had no protection and college life was a life of temptation. I was a star athlete being placed on a pedestal. I was 18 years old. I was invited to parties. I started drinking and using drugs. And along with that came the females and my first introduction to greed. Eventually, I gave in and started selling drugs. I was still able to continue my studies somehow, and graduated in 1975.

After returning to Denver, I played semi-professional basketball. I was doing well. Yet, I continued to sell and use cocaine and other drugs, a secret my family knew nothing about.

One day I was standing on my balcony in my downtown penthouse and thought, "There has to be something more to life than this. I know better than this." I struggled as soon as I started thinking about it, then I was right back to selling and using drugs. At times I thought I was on top of the world, and then down I went. I had an experience that caused me to reflect on my life. I found myself in a situation that goes along with the game. I thought I had shot someone in the head. When I turned around, the man's forehead had a crease—blood was gushing out. Although I had only grazed his head, fear came over me and I realized that I could have killed him.

As time went on, my dark side eventually caught up with me. I was arrested. My family bailed me out of jail. After going through the criminal process I was convicted. Upon going to court for sentencing the judge said he saw something in me that he normally didn't see in his courtroom. A young man with a college degree and a supporting cast of family and friends. I thought I was going to get probation, yet he sentenced me to 5-8 years. It was like the bubble had popped. I was going to prison and I was a preacher's kid. They handcuffed me and all my family couldn't believe it. I was transported from Denver County Jail to prison in Canon City, Colorado. The images I thought about prison were what I saw on TV. I couldn't believe it. I had a college degree and was playing basketball and I was going to jail.

After arriving at Territorial Prison, my reputation as a ball player and dope man came to light and other inmates wanted to be around me. The reality set in and I asked myself, "How can I adapt to this environment?" I began selling drugs and running a store out of my cell. I, basically, continued my negative lifestyle behind bars.

My parents visited me in prison. I never saw my mother cry before, but she cried. It pricked my spirit and I said, "Mom I am sorry." My mom said, "How can you say sorry after sending us all through this?" I replied, "Mom I am going to change but I really don't know how." She said, "Talk to God just like you talk to me." I battled with the conflict of how could I sell drugs and still call myself a Christian.

While in prison I saw horrible things. A man was raped and killed and that impacted me greatly. It still haunts me now. Another guy was stabbed and the blood gushed out of him. What could I have done to save these men? I am still hurting for them. I went back to my cell and prayed that God would work in me. I was remembering my mother's words. As I continued to pray it was as if a weight was lifted off of me. For me, mom's suggestion worked. It doesn't matter where you are. If you are sincere about it, you can do it. All of this led me to stop selling and I started leading Bible studies. Four people grew into forty. When the other inmates saw that I was sincere, it became a way of life. God was preparing me for his work.

I started taking a Bible study correspondence course to learn more about the Word of God. I asked myself "Who am I and what powers do I have." One Saturday I was called to the control center and was told to pack it up, "You are out of here." No one knew I was being released. When I showed up at home my family was so surprised, maybe they thought I had escaped. When I told them I was paroled early, they were overjoyed. I still had one package of cocaine stashed that I had kept to use when I got out to help me get back on my feet. As I retrieved the package, I thought about all the good times with drugs, but I knew I had to let it go. I opened the package and spread it on the ground and I said, "Satan I rebuke you in the name of Jesus, you have no more power over me." That was the last turning point in my life. I finally realized who I was. It all became very real to me.

There were many challenges I had to deal with now, being an ex-convict. Although I had always interviewed well, having a record changed everything. Potential employers never called back. I remember feeling the urge to give up, but something inside of me challenged me to continue. I went to another interview and I told myself that I have to do something different. I spoke candidly with the interviewer and told him, "I know my worth; my challenge is to prove to you what I am capable of. I will work for you for two weeks for free to prove to you that I would be an asset to your company. There would be nothing for you to lose." It was a recycling company.

The company agreed to try me out. I was told to be there at 8:00 a.m. and I arrived every day at 7:30 a.m. I was the first one to arrive and the last one to leave. At the end of the first week, the supervisor said, "Kelly, I want to see you. The first thought that came to my mind was that he was going to have to let me go since I wasn't being paid and it would be against company policy. But, he told me that he had noticed my work ethic and he thought I would be a valuable employee. I had proved my worth. He put me on the schedule for the following week and agreed to pay me for the week as well. Within one month, I became a supervisor.

In 1984, gangs really started migrating to Denver from California. Crips came to the east side of the city and Bloods claimed Park Hill, a neighborhood east of downtown. At the time I had become the athletic director at a local gym. I was able to establish relationships with the youth in the east side neighborhood including many gang members. When I started to experience firsthand the LA influence, I knew that in order to deal with this negative mind-set, I had to learn more. I went to Los Angeles, California to find out firsthand what Denver was in for. Upon returning to Denver, I attempted to warn the city fathers including the mayor and city council members in an effort to be pro-active. Their response about this potential plague was that they didn't want to cause panic. They wanted to take time to evaluate and analyze just how serious this problem was becoming. In the meantime, it continued to spread. The shootings in the beginning were meant to only intimidate. They now were hitting their marks, and kids were dying left and right.

Over time, the police and elected officials realized that we had a bigger problem on our hands than they originally thought. They needed me, just as much as the kids that were dying on the streets did. I finally realized that I was doing what God had prepared me to do.

Q: Any words to prisoners for encouragement?
Understand who they are in Christ and then be consistent when they get out. Challenges will come and they must be prepared for them.

Q: Any words to families of the incarcerated?
God has a way of putting out a stumbling block to get our attention and sometimes being locked up could be a blessing in disguise. If I hadn't been incarcerated, my life wouldn't have been changed so dramatically. I could have been killed, or worse, taken another's life. It gave me a wake-up call. Encourage your sons or daughters to ask themselves, "What am I supposed to learn from this? What is God saying to me? What's the message you want to give me?"

Q: Any words to a person who struggles with addiction?
Addiction has no respect for people. I was blessed that I didn't have to go through a physical rehab even though at times, I was doing $600 a day of drugs. But, for some users they need that kind of support. I did go through withdrawal and it affected me emotionally and physically, but again, I felt as though this was all part of my "Godly" training. So, ask yourself, "What is the purpose

of changing?" This question is important for those who want to change.

Q: What steps must a person take when they struggle with addiction?

Be true to yourself. Accept that you have a problem. Let go of your blame and take responsibility. Have faith in the Lord but understand that even though you may have all the faith in the world, without works, it is dead.

Q: Any miracles that you have experienced that you will never forget?

The first one that comes to my mind was when I was in my early 30's, and it was a Memorial Day weekend — I began hemorrhaging and spitting up blood. I ended up in the intensive care unit. I spent six days and after hearing the men of medicine say that they had done all that they could do, I thought, "What is going on?" God came to me and said, "I still have work for you to do." I realized that all of us are mortal. We all have a purpose. God had spared me again and had allowed me to continue my work of trying to save others.

Q: What are your regrets in life?

First of all, I regret disappointing my mom and dad with some of the decisions and actions that I made before going to prison. I realize that they forgave me a long time ago and through my good works I have been able to save many. It's still hard for a son, to remember the pain in his parent's eyes and know that he was responsible.

Secondly, I still struggle with forgiving myself. I realize that if I hadn't had the journey that I did, I wouldn't be the man I am today. A pastor reminded me that God forgives us before we are even born. And, the State forgave me in 2010 when the governor granted me an official pardon. Yet, I still regret the lives that I touched negatively. I always say that I don't condone the negative actions of some of the youth I deal with, but I value their lives. Above all, I have learned how precious and yet, fleeting life is.

Part Four:
How to Start Prisoner's Book Project

This is for those who are interested in starting a prisoner's book project similar to *Maximum Saints* books. Some chaplains and volunteers who saw the impact of *Maximum Saints* books asked me how they can start a similar project. Here is the step by step method Transformation Project Prison Ministry (TPPM) took and you can adopt any areas according to your need.

(1) Find a facility where they are open to this project: Ask the inmates to write their stories and edit the stories of other inmates, this encourages the inmates and is good for the facility. Many times inmates have spare time and don't know what to do. If you can convince your chaplain or program department that this will help the inmates and the facility, they will be more open to support this kind of project. Call it a "Writing project for inmates who have experienced transformation."

(2) Find a chaplain or a volunteer who would be committed to gathering stories for this project: You have to work with a person who is committed to gathering stories and then others can help with typing and editing. Find stories that will help others and stories about how God has helped them in their difficult times.

(3) Find a name for this project and create a professional looking brochure: Once people understand your mission and service they will want to donate to your project. You will need to include a section in your brochure with instruction on where to send donations.

(4) You can start a non-profit corporation or find a church that will support your project. I didn't start with non-profit status right away because of the cost involved. I also wasn't sure how this project would go. In addition, I didn't want to keep track of all the funds, so I decided to find a church. Broomfield United Methodist Church handled the funds and later Park Hill United Methodist church did. Then when I met Laura Nokes-Lang, she

started non-profit for TPPM.

(5) Create a consent form: God blessed TPPM with a lawyer who created a consent form to protect TPPM from those who want to use their stories for their own selfish reasons other than helping others or giving God glory by sharing their stories and art work. TPPM does not pay anyone for writing their stories and paying inmates is against the policy of the facility. Also, TPPM does not let inmates use donated material to gain court favor. Anyone can write to their judge for their case, but when they donate material it is to give God glory and to help others by sharing how God helped them. That is to protect the integrity of our mission. So, find a good lawyer who can help you to create a consent form for your organization.

(6) Make sure your mission is clear: The TPPM mission is to share the love of Jesus Christ through the stories of transformation. I see it two ways: 1) Help people find Christ so they can be saved and find direction in life. 2) To help people grow spiritually so they can help others. Inmates' testimonies are so powerful and God can use them to convert and help others grow in faith. Our focus is clear so it's easy for us to know which story we need to add to the book.

(7) You need to find someone who can convert your typed text into book format: Find a graphic designer for the book cover: Encourage inmates to draw for the book cover.

(8) Find a publisher which will be reasonable. We self-publish books and we worked with the following company: RR Donnelley, RR Donnelley & Sons, N9234 Lake Park Road, Appleton, WI 54915 (920) 969-6427. You have to provide all the text and cover in PDF format.

(9) Keep working on fundraising project: TPPM is an interdenominational project. I visited many different churches across denominations. I preached, shared and gave mission presentation to promote this project and people started to donate. The first three years, I was visiting an average of more than 20 churches and organizations every year. Keep knocking on the doors and praying so the Holy Spirit will lead you to where you need to go.

(10) Work with a connection system if you can: Funding is very crucial for this project. I am a United Methodist minister and I

feel very fortunate that United Methodist is a connectional system and they approved TPPM project as a mission project. Still, if this project is only supported by United Methodist churches, our mission is limited. That's why I work with many different churches and denominations and organizations.

(11) Contact local media and newspaper companies to see if they want to help you promote your project. Ask them if they want to interview and write an article about your project.

APPENDICES

An Invitation

AN INVITATION TO ACCEPT CHRIST – Words of invitation from the F Module Pod 1300 & Prayer written by D Module Pod 5 Maximum Saints from the ACDF.

Are you questioning God? Do you lift your hands in frustration and cry? Have you created an unbearable amount of pain in your life that you cannot handle? Are loved ones on the outside reaching out to you, but they can no longer touch you? Is there an incredible emptiness and pain in your stomach that no one understands? A pain that no one can take away? No more questioning: Now is the time to act! Do not delay!! Bow down. Let the One who created the world lift your burdens and cleanse your soul. Let Jesus' love, hope, and joy fill you to the maximum. Jesus can help you deal with pain when no one else can. He can give you peace when no one else can. Here is a prayer that you can pray (if you would like to invite Christ into your heart), so you can be saved and experience the peace of Christ in your heart.

"Dear Jesus,

I am prepared to invite you into my heart, mind, body, and soul. I come before you offering myself as a living sacrifice, confessing my sins and weaknesses. Father, I put all of my trust in you, and I want You to have total control over my life. I am sorry, Lord, for the things I have done that grieve you and others. Please forgive me for all of my sins. I ask that the distractions around me be put on hold so that I will be able to receive you into my life today. Please send your Holy Spirit into my heart, and give me the power to live a new life in Christ. Thank you, Lord, for your love. I give my life to you in the name of Jesus. Amen"

"If you confess with your mouth, 'Jesus is Lord,' and believe in your heart that God raised Him from the dead you will be saved." (Romans 10:9)
"If we confess our sins, he is faithful and just and will forgive us our sins and purify us from all unrighteousness." (1 John 1:9)
"Jesus answered, 'I am the way and the truth and the life. No one comes to the Father except through me." (John 14:6)

An invitation for The Transformation Project Prison Ministry (TPPM):
Books and DVDs produced by TPPM are distributed in many jails, prisons and homeless shelters nationwide free of charge made possible by grants and donations. America has 2.3 million people incarcerated, the largest prison population in the world. There is a great shortage of inspirational books in many jails and prisons.

"One Million Dream Project"
    In 2010, TPPM board decided to expand the ministry goal, and started the "One Million Dream Project." TPPM decided to raise enough funds to distribute one million copies of each book that TPPM has produced for prisoners and homeless people. I ask you to pray for this project so God can help TPPM to reach out to those who cannot speak for themselves and are in need of spiritual guidance. TPPM is a 501(c)(3) nonprofit organization, so your donation is 100% tax deductible. If you would like to be a partner in this very important mission of bringing transformation through the message of Christ in prisons and homeless shelters, or want to know more about this project, please visit: www.maximumsaints.org. You can donate on line or you can write a check addressed to:
Transformation Project Prison Ministry
    5209 Montview Boulevard
    Denver, CO 80207

Website: www.maximumsaints.org
Facebook: http://tinyurl.com/yhhcp5g

How to purchase *Maximum Saints* books:
This is for individuals who would like to purchase or send a copy to their incarcerated family. TPPM receives lots of requests for individual distribution but we only distribute them through chaplains. All the proceeds from *Maximum Saints* will go to TPPM to distribute more free books and DVDs to prisons and homeless shelters.
To find out more about purchasing *Maximum Saints* books,

check our website: www.maximumsaints.org. The
following books are available:

Book One: *Maximum Saints Never Hide in the Dark*
Book Two: *Maximum Saints Make No Little Plans*
Book Three: *Maximum Saints Dream*
Book Four: *Maximum Saints Forgive*
Book Five: *Maximum Saints All Things Are Possible*

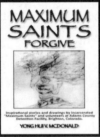

About The Author

Yong Hui V. McDonald, also known as Vescinda McDonald, is a chaplain at Adams County Detention Facility (ACDF) in Brighton, Colorado. She is a certified American Correctional chaplain, spiritual director and on-call hospital chaplain.

She is the founder of the following:
- Transformation Project Prison Ministry (TPPM), a 501 (c)(3) non-profit, in 2005. TPPM produces Maximum Saints books and DVDs of ACDF saints stories of transformation and they are distributed freely to prisons, and homeless shelters. Website: www.transformprisons.org
- GriefPathway Ventures LLC, in 2010, to produce books, DVDs, and audio books to help others to process grief and healing. Website: www.griefpathway.com
- Veterans Twofish Foundation, a 501(c)(3) nonprofit organization, produces, publishes, and distributes stories of veterans and veterans' families. They provide educational and emotional support and encouragement to veterans and their families through chaplains services. Website: www.veteranstwofish.org

Education:
- Multnomah University, B.A.B.E. (1984)
- Iliff School of Theology, Master of Divinity (2002)

Books and Audio Books by Yong Hui:
- *Journey With Jesus, Visions, Dreams, Meditations & Reflections*
- *Dancing in the Sky, A Story of Hope for Grieving Hearts*
- *Twisted Logic, The Shadow of Suicide*
- *Twisted Logic, The Window of Depression*
- *Dreams & Interpretations, Healing from Nightmares*
- *I Was The Mountain, In Search of Faith & Revival*
- *The Ultimate Parenting Guide, How to Enjoy Peaceful*

Parenting and Joyful Children
- *Tornadoes of War, Inspirational Stories of Veterans and Veteran's Families,* under the Veterans Twofish Foundation
- *Prisoners Victory Parade, Extraordinary Stories of Maximum Saints & Former Prisoners*
- *Four Voices, How They Affect Our Mind: How to Overcome Self-Destructive Voices and Hear the Nurturing Voice of God*
- *Tornadoes, Grief, Loss, Trauma, and PTSD: Tornadoes, Lessons and Teachings—The TLT Model for Healing*
- *Prayer and Meditations, 12 Prayer Projects for Spiritual Growth and Healing*
- *Invisible Counselor, Amazing Stories of the Holy Spirit*
- *Tornadoes of Accidents, Finding Peace in Tragic Accidents*
- Complied and published *Tornadoes of War, Inspirational Stories of Veterans and Veteran's Families* under the Veterans Twofish Foundation
- Compiled and published five *Maximum Saints* books under the Transformation Project Prison Ministry.

DVDs produced by Yong Hui:
- *Dancing in The Sky, Mismatched Shoes*
- *Tears of The Dragonfly, Suicide and Suicide Prevention (Audio CD* is also available*)*

Spanish books by Yong Hui:
- *Twisted Logic, The Shadow of Suicide*
- *Journey With Jesus, Visions, Dreams, Meditations and Reflections*

GriefPathway Ventures, LLC.
P.O. Box 220
Brighton, CO 80601
Website: www.griefpathway.com